education
and training

The Career Ideas for Teens Series

CAREER IDEAS for teens in

education and training

Diane Lindsey Reeves
and Kelly Gunzenhauser

Ferguson's
An Infobase Learning Company

East Baton Rouge Parish Library
Baton Rouge, Louisiana

Career Ideas for Teens in Education and Training

Ferguson's
An imprint of Infobase Learning
132 West 31st Street
New York NY 10001

Library of Congress Cataloging-in-Publication Data
Reeves, Diane Lindsey, 1959-
Career ideas for teens in education and training / Diane Lindsey Reeves and Kelly Gunzenhauser. — 2nd ed.
        p. cm. — (Career Ideas for Teens)
    Includes bibliographical references and index.
    ISBN-13: 978-0-8160-8274-2 (hardcover : alk. paper)
    ISBN-10: 0-8160-8274-X (hardcover : alk. paper) 1. Teaching—Vocational guidance—Juvenile literature. 2. Training—Vocational guidance—Juvenile literature. 3. Education—Vocational guidance—Juvenile literature. 4. Teenagers—Life skills guides—Juvenile literature. I. Gunzenhauser, Kelly. II. Title.
    LB1775.R417 2012
    370.23—dc23   2011023906

Ferguson's books are available at special discounts when purchased in bulk quantities for businesses, associations, institutions, or sales promotions. Please call our Special Sales Department in New York at (212) 967-8800 or (800) 322-8755.

You can find Ferguson's on the World Wide Web at http://www.infobaselearning.com

Text design and composition by Annie O'Donnell
Cover design by Takeshi Takahashi
Illustrations by Matt Wood
Cover printed by Yurchak Printing, Landisville, Pa.
Book printed and bound by Yurchak Printing, Landisville, Pa.
Printed in the United States of America

This book is printed on acid-free paper.

CONTENTS

Welcome to Your Future

Q: What is one of the most dreaded questions of the high school experience?

A: What are you going to do after you graduate?

Talk about pressure! You have to come up with an answer sometime soon. But, homecoming is right around the corner; coach called an extra practice; homework is piling up....

Feel free to delay the inevitable. But here's the deal: Sooner or later the same people who make you go to school now are eventually going to make you stop. If you get it right, you'll exit with diploma in hand and at least a general idea of what to do next.

So...

What *are* you going to do after you graduate?

There are plenty of choices. You could go away to college or give community college a try; get a job or enlist in the military. Maybe you can convince your parents to bankroll an extended break to travel the world. Or, perhaps, you want to see what's out there by volunteering for a favorite cause or interning with an interesting company.

Of course, you may be one of the lucky few who have always known what they wanted to do with their lives—be a doctor, chef, or whatever. All you need to do is figure out a few wheres, whens, and hows to get you on your way. Get the training, master the skills, and off you go to fulfill your destiny.

On the other hand, you may be one of the hordes of high schoolers who have absolutely no clue what they want to do with the rest of their lives. But—whatever—you'll just head off to college anyway. After all, everyone else is doing it. And, for that matter, everyone that matters seems to think that's what you're *supposed* to do.

But, here's the thing: College is pretty much a once-in-a-lifetime opportunity. Not to mention that it is a *very expensive* once-in-a-lifetime-opportunity. It's unlikely that you'll ever get another four years to step back from the rest of the world and totally focus on getting yourself ready to succeed in life. Assuming that you are way too smart to squander your best shot at success with aimless dabbling, you can use this book to make well-informed choices about your future.

A premise suggested by a famous guy named Noel Coward inspired the ultimate goal of this book. Coward was an English playwright who was born in 1899. After a colorful life working as a composer, director, actor, and singer, Coward concluded that interesting "work is more fun than fun." Making this statement true for you is what this book is all about.

Mind you, fun isn't limited to the ha-ha, goofing-off-with-friends variety. Sometimes it's best expressed as the big sigh of satisfaction people describe when they truly enjoy their life's work. It involves finding the kind of work that provides purpose to your days and a solid foundation for building a well-rounded life. You'll know you've found it when you look forward to Mondays almost as much as you do Fridays!

Need more convincing? Consider this: If you are like most people, you will spend a big chunk of the next 40 or 50 years of your life working. Sorry to break it to you like that but, well, welcome to the real world. Putting a little thought into how you really want to spend all that time kind of makes sense, doesn't it?

If you agree, you've come to the right place. In these pages you'll encounter a sequence of activities and strategies you can use—much like a compass—to find your way to a bright future. Each of the 16 titles in the *Career Ideas for Teens* series features the following three sections:

SECTION ONE: DISCOVER YOU AT WORK

It's your choice, your career, your future. Do you notice a common theme here? Yep, this first step is all about you. Stop here and

> ## REALITY CHECK
> News flash! Contrary to popular opinion, you cannot grow up to be anything you want to be. You can, however, grow up to be anything you are willing to work hard to become.

WHICH WAY SHOULD YOU GO?

Each of the 16 titles in the *Career Ideas for Teens* series focuses on a specific industry theme. Some people refer to these themes as career "clusters." Others call them career "pathways." Your school may even offer career academies based on one or more of these themes. Whatever you call them, they offer a terrific way to explore the entire world of work in manageable, easy-to-navigate segments. Explore *Career Ideas for Teens* in...

- Agriculture, Food, and Natural Resources
- Architecture and Construction
- Arts and Communications
- Business, Management, and Administration
- Education and Training
- Finance
- Government and Public Service
- Health Science
- Hospitality and Tourism
- Human Services
- Information Technology
- Law and Public Safety
- Manufacturing
- Marketing
- Science, Technology, Engineering, and Math
- Transportation, Distribution, and Logistics

think about what you really want to do. Better yet, stick around until you get a sense of the skills, interests, ambitions, and values you already possess that can take you places in the real world.

Sure, this first step can be a doozy. It's also one that many people miss. Just talk to the adults in your life about their career choices. Find out how many of them took the time to choose a career based on personal preferences and strengths. Then ask how many of them wish now that they had. You're likely to learn that if they had it to do over again, they would jump at the chance to make well-informed career choices.

SECTION TWO: EXPLORE YOUR OPTIONS

Next, come all the career ideas you'd expect to find in a book called *Career Ideas for Teens*. Each of the 35 careers featured in this section represents possible destinations along a career cluster pathway. With opportunities associated with 16 different career clusters—everything from agriculture and art to transportation and technology—you're sure to find intriguing new ideas to consider. Forget any preconceived notions about what you (or others) think you *should* be and take some time to figure out what you really want to be. Put all the things you discovered about yourself in Section One to good use as you explore the world of work.

SECTION THREE: EXPERIMENT WITH SUCCESS

What would it really be like to be a...whatever it is you want to be? Why wait until it's too late to change your mind to find out? Here's your chance to take career ideas of interest for a test drive. Play around with this one; give that one a try.... It's a no-pressure, no-obligation way to find work you really want to do.

This three-step process is about uncovering potential (yours) and possibilities (career paths). Plunge in, give it some thought, uncover the clues, put the pieces together...whatever it takes to find the way to your very best future!

DISCOVER YOU AT WORK

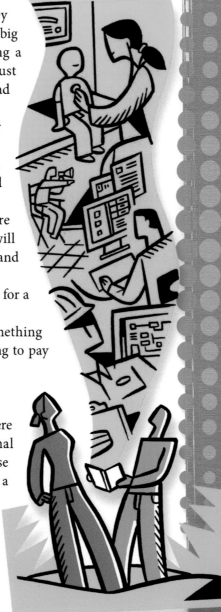

Sometimes people make things harder than they have to be. Like waiting until the night before a big exam to start studying.... Agonizing over asking a special someone to the prom instead of, um, just asking.... Worrying about finishing a project instead of sitting down and doing it....

Figuring out what you want to do with your life can be that way, too. Sure, it is a big decision. And, yes, the choices you make now can have a big impact on the rest of your life. But, there's good news. You don't have to figure everything out now.

Bottom line, every potential employer you are likely to encounter throughout your entire career will want to know two things: "What do you know?" and "What can you do?"

That being the case, what can you do to prepare for a successful career?

Two things: 1) Become a skilled expert in something that you like to do, and 2) find an employer willing to pay you to do it.

Really.

It's that simple...and that complicated.

"Me, Myself, and I" offers a starting point where you can uncover insightful clues about personal interests, skills, values, and ambitions you can use to make sound career decisions. Think through a round of who, what, when, where, how questions in "Me, Myself, and I" about you and then move on to "Hello, World of Work," where you'll discover how to match what you want from work with what specific types of skills employers need from you.

SOME GOOD ADVICE

"If you want an average successful life, it doesn't take much planning. Just stay out of trouble, go to school, and apply for jobs you might like. But if you want something extraordinary, you have two choices:

1. Become the best at one specific thing.
2. Become very good (top 25 percent) at two or more things.

The first strategy is difficult to the point of near impossibility. Few people will ever play in the NBA or make a platinum album. I don't recommend anyone even try.

The second strategy is fairly easy. Everyone has at least a few areas in which they could be in the top 25 percent with some effort. In my case, I can draw better than most people can, but I'm hardly an artist. And I'm not any funnier than the average standup comedian who never makes it big, but I'm funnier than most people. The magic is that few people can draw well and write jokes. It's the combination of the two that makes what I do so rare. And when you add in my business background, suddenly I had a topic that few cartoonists could hope to understand without living it."

—*Scott Adams,*
creator of the Dilbert *comic strip*

Me, Myself, and I

Why do I need to learn all this stuff? Chances are that at some point in the dozen or so years you have already spent in school you have asked this question a time or two. Come on. What can quadratic polynomials and the periodic table of elements possibly have to do with the rest of your life?

Among other things, your education is supposed to get you ready to succeed in the real world. Yes, all those grammar rules and mathematical mysteries will someday come in handy no matter what you end up doing. Nevertheless, more than all the facts and figures you've absorbed, the plan all along—from kindergarten to graduation—has been to make sure you learn how to learn.

If you know how to learn, you'll know how to seek out and acquire pretty much anything you need or want to know. Get the knowledge, gain the skills, and the resulting expertise is your ticket to a successful career.

As its title suggests, this chapter is all about you—and for a very good reason. Your traits, interests, skills, work style, and values offer important clues you can use to make important decisions about your future—for valid reasons with intention and purpose.

And, speaking of clues…

Think of yourself like a good mystery, but instead of sleuthing out whodunit, focus on collecting evidence about you. By the time you have completed the following six activities, you'll be ready to encounter the world of work on your own terms.

Discover #1: WHO Am I?
Discover #2: WHAT Do I Like to Do?
Discover #3: WHERE Does My Work Style Fit Best?
Discover #4: WHY Do My Work Values Matter?
Discover #5: HOW Ready Am I for the 21st-Century Workplace?
Discover #6: "Me" Résumé

ON SUCCESS
If you don't know what you want, how will you know when you get it?

ON LIFE DIRECTION
If you don't know where you are going, how will you know when you get there?

DISCOVER #1: WHO AM I?

Make a grid with three columns and six rows on a blank sheet of paper. Number each row from one to six.

- In the first row, write the three best words you'd use to describe yourself.
- In the second row, ask a good friend what three words they'd use to describe you.
- In the third row, ask a favorite teacher for three words that she thinks best describe you.
  - In the fourth row, ask a coach, club adviser, youth leader, or other adult mentor to use three words to describe you.
  - In the fifth row, ask a sibling or other young relative to take a crack at describing you.
  - In the sixth row, ask a parent or trusted adult relative for three descriptive words about you.

You			
Friend			
Teacher			
Coach or mentor			
Sibling or young relative			
Parent or adult relative			

Discovery #1: I Am...

Look for common themes in the way that others see you and compare them with the way you see yourself. Include the words used most often to describe you to write an official, ready-for-*Merriam-Webster's-Dictionary* definition of you.

_____

_____

_____

DISCOVER #2: WHAT DO I LIKE TO DO?

Think fast! Use a blank sheet of paper to complete the following statements with the first answers that come to mind.

1 I like to _____ , _____ ,

and _____ .

2 I am really good at _____ ,

_____ , and _____ .

3 I totally suck at _____ , _____ ,

and _____ .

4 Something I can do for hours without getting bored is

_____ .

5 One thing that absolutely bores me to tears is

_____ .

6 My favorite subjects in school are _____ ,

_____ , and _____ .

7 In my free time, I especially like to _____ ,

_____ , and _____ .

8 Something I'd really like to learn how to do is

_____ .

9 Other people compliment me most often about

_____ .

Discovery #2: I Like…

Use your responses to the prompts above to create a list of your
three top interests. See if you can identify off the top of your head
at least three careers with a direct connection to each interest.

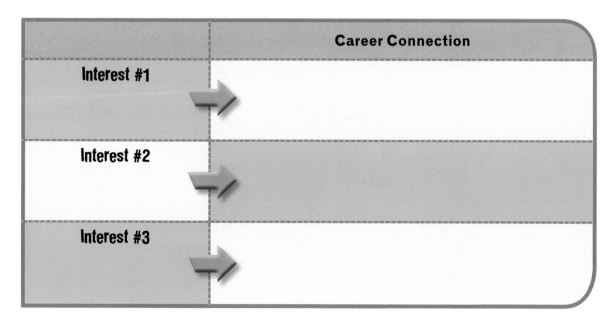

	Career Connection
Interest #1	
Interest #2	
Interest #3	

DISCOVER #3: WHERE DOES MY WORK STYLE FIT BEST?

It is your first day on the job and it's time for lunch. Walking into the employee cafeteria, you discover six tables. There is a big welcome sign instructing new employees to find the table that best matches his or her style. You quickly conclude that they aren't talking about preppy or retro fashions and start looking for other things you share in common. Read the following descriptions and choose the table where you fit in best.

Table 1: The Doers

These people do what it takes to get the job done, whether it involves building, fixing, or growing things, training people, or playing sports. They are practical, hands-on problem solvers who especially enjoy the great outdoors. Forget the paperwork and keep the human interaction to a minimum—these people would rather do something than talk about it. Among the colleagues seated at this table are an aerospace engineer, architect, carpenter, chef, civil engineer, park ranger, and police officer.

Table 2: The Thinkers

These people have never met a fact they didn't like. With a preference for tasks that require mental acuity over physical activity, you're likely to encounter as many laptops as lunchboxes here. Well known for insatiable curiosity, be prepared to answer lots of questions, discuss off-the-wall-subjects, and take a shot at the latest brainteaser circulating around the table. Feel free to strike up a conversation with your pick of an archaeologist, chiropractor, computer programmer, electrician, ecologist, psychologist, or zoologist.

ORGANIZER

HELPER

THINKER

DOER

CREATOR

PERSUADER

TAKE A SEAT!

A few things you'll want to know about these "lunch tables":

1. Each "table" represents one of the widely used Holland codes. This classification system was developed by psychologist Dr. John Holland as a way to link six distinct personality types to career choices and work success. The official work personality types include:
   - Doers = Realistic (R)
   - Thinkers = Investigative (I)
   - Creators = Artistic (A)
   - Helpers = Social (S)
   - Persuaders = Enterprising (E)
   - Organizers = Conventional (C)

2. There is no "best" work personality. It takes all kinds to keep the world working. When everything is in balance, there's a job for every person and a person for every job.

3. You, like most people, are probably a unique combination of more than one personality type: a little of this, a lot of that. That's what makes people interesting.

You can go online, plug in your work personality codes, and find lists of interest-related career options at http://online.onetcenter.org/find/descriptor/browse/Interests.

Table 3: The Creators

Here you'll find the artsy, free-spirit types—those drawn to words, art, and other forms of creative self-expression. Rules and structure tend to box in these out-of-the-box thinkers. Doing their own thing

WHAT'S YOUR STYLE?

ARE YOU A DOER?

Are you:
- Independent?
- Reserved?
- Practical?
- Mechanical?
- Athletic?
- Persistent?

Do you like:
- Building things?
- Training animals?
- Playing sports?
- Fixing things?
- Gardening?
- Hunting?
- Fishing?

ARE YOU A THINKER?

Are you:
- Logical?
- Independent?
- Analytical?
- Observant?
- Inquisitive?

Do you like:
- Exploring new subjects?
- Doing puzzles?
- Messing around with computers?
- Solving mysteries?
- Keeping up with the latest news and world events?
- Tackling new challenges?

ARE YOU A CREATOR?

Are you:
- Imaginative?
- Intuitive?
- Expressive?
- Emotional?
- Creative?
- Independent?

Do you like:
- Drawing?
- Painting?
- Playing an instrument?
- Visiting museums?
- Acting?
- Designing clothes ?
- Decorating spaces?
- Reading?
- Traveling?
- Writing?

ARE YOU A HELPER?

Are you:
- Friendly?
- Outgoing?
- Empathic?
- Persuasive?
- Idealistic?
- Generous?

Do you like:
- Joining clubs?
- Playing team sports?
- Caring for children?
- Going to parties?
- Meeting new people?

ARE YOU A PERSUADER?

Are you:
- Assertive?
- Self-confident?
- Ambitious?
- Extroverted?
- Optimistic?
- Adventurous?

Do you like:
- Organizing parties and other events?
- Selling things?
- Promoting ideas?
- Giving speeches?
- Starting businesses?

ARE YOU AN ORGANIZER?

Are you:
- Well-organized?
- Accurate?
- Practical?
- Persistent?
- Conscientious?
- Ambitious?

Do you like:
- Working with numbers?
- Collecting or organizing things?
- Proofreading?
- Keeping records?
- Keeping yourself and others on track?

MY WORK STYLE(S) IS...

- ❑ Doer (Realistic)
- ❑ Helper (Social)
- ❑ Thinker (Investigative)
- ❑ Persuader (Enterprising)
- ❑ Creator (Artistic)
- ❑ Organizer (Conventional)

is what they do best. Among your potential lunch companions are an actor, cartoon animator, choreographer, drama teacher, fashion designer, graphic designer, interior designer, journalist, and writer.

Table 4: Helpers

Good luck trying to get a word in edgewise at this table. Helpers are "people" people: always ready for a good chat or to lend a helping hand. Communicating with others trumps working with objects, machines, or data. They are all about serving people, promoting learning, and making the world a better place. Sit down and get acquainted with an arbitrator, art therapist, childcare worker, coach, counselor, cruise director, fitness trainer, registered nurse, and teacher.

Table 5: The Persuaders

While helpers focus on helping people, persuaders are natural leaders or managers—especially adept at getting people to do what they want them to do. These people are more about action than analysis, equally comfortable with taking risks and responsibility. Entrepreneurs at heart, they like to make things happen. Sit down and find your place among peers such as an advertising executive, criminal investigator, lawyer, lobbyist, school principal, stockbroker, and urban planner.

Table 6: The Organizers

Organizers are people you can count on to cross their t's and dot their i's. In other words, no detail escapes their careful attention. Most comfortable doing things "by the book," organizers thrive on routine and structure. A penchant for following instructions and respecting authority gives these types something of a squeaky-clean reputation. Make yourself comfortable and enjoy a nice break with an accountant, actuary, air traffic controller, chief financial officer, economist, mathematician, and paralegal.

DISCOVER #4: WHY DO MY WORK VALUES MATTER?

There's another thing to consider before evaluating all of the clues you've gathered. According to O*Net OnLine, America's primary source of occupational information, six types of values are commonly associated with workplace satisfaction: achievement, independence, recognition, relationships, support, and working conditions. Read each of the following statements and put an X in the box preceding those that are important to you.

In considering my future career, it matters most that

- ❑ **1.** I make use of my abilities.
- ❑ **2.** I can try out my own ideas.
- ❑ **3.** I can give directions and instructions to others.
- ❑ **4.** I would never be pressured to do things that go against my sense of right and wrong.
- ❑ **5.** I would be treated fairly by the company.
- ❑ **6.** The job would provide for steady employment.
- ❑ **7.** I enjoy the satisfaction of a job well done.
- ❑ **8.** I can make decisions on my own.
- ❑ **9.** I could receive recognition for the work I do.
- ❑ **10.** I could do things for other people.
- ❑ **11.** I have supervisors who would support their workers with management.
- ❑ **12.** My pay would compare well with that of other workers.
- ❑ **13.** What I do matters.
- ❑ **14.** I can work with little supervision.
- ❑ **15.** The job would provide an opportunity for advancement.
- ❑ **16.** My coworkers would be easy to get along with.
- ❑ **17.** I have supervisors who train their workers well.
- ❑ **18.** The job would have good working conditions.

- ❏ **19.** I find a sense of accomplishment in my work.
- ❏ **20.** I have some flexibility in when and how I do my work.
- ❏ **21.** My work efforts are appreciated.
- ❏ **22.** I have the opportunity to work with all kinds of people.
- ❏ **23.** My work expectations are clearly defined and necessary resources are provided.
- ❏ **24.** I could do something different every day.

Tally up your results here.

Achievement	Independence	Recognition
❏ 1	❏ 2	❏ 3
❏ 7	❏ 8	❏ 9
❏ 13	❏ 14	❏ 15
❏ 19	❏ 20	❏ 21
Total	**Total**	**Total**
Relationships	**Support**	**Working Conditions**
❏ 4	❏ 5	❏ 6
❏ 10	❏ 11	❏ 12
❏ 16	❏ 17	❏ 18
❏ 22	❏ 23	❏ 24
Total	**Total**	**Total**

Your Work Values at Work

Once you've clued yourself in to what's important to you in a career, you need to connect those values to actual jobs.

Achievement: If Achievement is your highest work value, look for jobs that let you use your best abilities. Look for work where you can see the results of your efforts. Explore jobs where you can get a genuine sense of accomplishment.

Independence: If Independence is your highest work value, look for jobs where employers let you do things on your own initiative. Explore work where you can make decisions on your own.

Recognition: If Recognition is your highest work value, explore jobs that come with good possibilities for advancement. Look for work with prestige or with the potential for leadership.

Relationships: If Relationships are your highest work value, look for jobs where your coworkers are friendly. Look for work that lets you be of service to others. Explore jobs that do not make you do anything that goes against your sense of right and wrong.

Support: If Support is your highest work value, look for jobs where the company stands behind its workers and where supervision is handled in supportive ways. Explore work in companies with a reputation for competent, considerate, and fair management.

Working Conditions: If Working Conditions are your highest work value, consider pay, job security, and good working conditions when looking at jobs. Look for work that suits your work style. Some people like to be busy all the time, or work alone, or have many different things to do.

Discovery #4: My Work Values Include

- ❏ Achievement
- ❏ Independence
- ❏ Recognition
- ❏ Relationships
- ❏ Support
- ❏ Working Conditions

DISCOVER #5: HOW READY AM I FOR THE 21ST-CENTURY WORKPLACE?

Are you ready for the 21st-century workforce? Some of America's most prominent employers and educators want to make sure. They put their heads together and came up with a list of essential skills, called 21st-century skills, which they recommend you bring to your first big job.

Some of these skills you've been busy acquiring without even knowing it. For instance, every time you go online to play games or do a little social networking you are cultivating important technology skills. Other skills will take some work. You can find an official description of these skills at http://www.p21.org. In the meantime, you can do a very informal assessment of your workplace skills using this 21st-century skills meter.

21st-CENTURY SKILLS METER

On the following scales, 1 represents total cluelessness, 10 represents impressive competency of the straight-A variety, and 2–9 represent varying degrees in between

How would you describe your mastery of the following subject:

	1	2	3	4	5	6	7	8	9	10
English, reading, and language arts?										
Foreign language?										
Arts?										
Mathematics?										
Economics?										
Science?										
Geography?										
History?										
Government and civics?										

How would you rate your current knowledge about:

	1	2	3	4	5	6	7	8	9	10
Global issues?										
Other cultures, religions, and lifestyles?										
Managing your personal finances?										
Understanding the world of work?										
Using entrepreneurial skills to enhance workplace productivity and career options?										

(continues)

21st-CENTURY SKILLS METER *(continued)*

	1	2	3	4	5	6	7	8	9	10
Local and national political events?										
Being part of the democratic process?										
Making good choices about your health and wellness?										
How good are you at:										
Making good decisions using sound judgment based on careful evaluation of evidence and ideas?										
Solving problems using both common sense and innovative ideas?										
Communicating thoughts and ideas verbally?										
Communicating thoughts and ideas in writing?										
Using various types of media and technology to inform, instruct, motivate, and/or persuade?										
Collaborating with others and working as a team?										

21st-CENTURY SKILLS METER

	1	2	3	4	5	6	7	8	9	10
Finding information in a wide variety of ways that includes books, newspapers, the Internet, etc.?										
Quickly learning how to use new technologies such as smart phones and online games?										
Getting used to new situations and finding the middle ground in disagreements?										
Thinking "out of the box" in creative and innovative ways?										
Understanding world issues and global cultures?										
Finding ways to protect and sustain the earth's environment?										

Discovery #5: I Am Getting Ready for the 21st-Century Workforce...

Use the two columns below to list skills you are already actively cultivating (those you scored 6 or higher) and those you need to take steps to pursue (those you scored 5 or lower).

In Progress	In Pursuit

DISCOVER #6: "ME" RÉSUMÉ

Eventually you will need to put together a job-hunting résumé that presents in a concise and compelling way all the reasons an employer should hire you. But, you aren't looking for a job right now. You are looking for a future.

It just so happens that creating a résumé with a twist offers a great way to make sense of all the fascinating facts you've just discovered about yourself. It also offers the double-whammy benefit of practicing your résumé-writing skills. So use the following format to create a "me" résumé summarizing what you've just learned about yourself in a professional way.

NAME
I am...
(* Put the definition of you here)
I like...
(* Key interests)
I work best...
(* Work style)
I most value...
(* Work values)
I am getting ready for the 21st-century workforce...
(* 21st-century skills already acquired and in process)

Hello, World of Work

Pop quiz!

What are the two things necessary for finding a successful career?

Hint #1: You started thinking about some interesting options for one of these "ingredients" in "Me, Myself, and I."

Hint #2: You are about to find out how to find the second ingredient in "Hello, World of Work."

Give yourself an A+ if your answer is anything like

1 Become an expert in something that you like to do, and
2 Find an employer who is willing to pay you to do it.

Finding a career you want to pursue is only half the challenge. The flipside involves finding out what the world of work wants from you. Keep the clues you discovered about yourself in the "Me, Myself, and I" section in the back of your mind as the focus shifts from self-discovery to work-discovery.

It's a big world out there—finding a path where you can get where you want to go is the next order of business.

DISCOVER #7: WHERE CAN MY INTERESTS AND SKILLS TAKE ME?

First, a confession: The following interest inventory is intended for use as an informal career exploration tool. It makes no claims of scientific validity or statistical reliability.

It was inspired by (and used with permission of) the Career Clusters Interest Survey developed by the States' Career Clusters Initiative, and the Oklahoma Department of Career and Technology Education. It includes significant revisions, however, that are meant to offer an age-appropriate, self-discovery tool to teens like you.

Your school guidance office can provide information about formal assessment and aptitude resources you may want to use at some point. In the meantime, use this informal interest inventory to start your exploration process and to make the connection between you and the world of work.

Following are eight different lists representing diverse interests that range from childhood play preferences to save-the-world ambitions. Each type of interest offers unique insight about career paths that may take you where you want to go in life.

Read each question and choose the response(s) that are most true for you.

When you were a little kid, what was your favorite thing to do?

❏ 1. Play outside, explore nature, plan big adventures.

❏ 2. Build things with Lego's, Lincoln logs, or other construction sets.

❏ 3. Put on plays to entertain your family and friends.

❏ 4. Run a lemonade stand.

❏ 5. Pretend you were a teacher and play school.

❏ 6. Play storekeeper and run the cash register with phony money.

❏ 7. Pretend you were president of the United States or boss of the world.

❏ 8. Play doctor and nurse your stuffed animals and siblings back to health.

❏ 9. Get your friends and neighbors together for backyard games, obstacle courses, or secret clubs.

❏ 10. Take care of stray animals, play with pets, pet-sit for neighbors.

❏ 11. Play Nintendo, Game Boy, or other kinds of video games.

❏ 12. Take turns being the "bad guy" in cops and robbers or use a spy kit to collect fingerprints and other clues.

❏ 13. Build model planes or cars or come up with new inventions.

❏ 14. Do arts and crafts.

❑ **15.** Concoct new formulas with a junior chemistry set.

❑ **16.** Play with cars, trucks, and trains, and build roads and bridges.

Which of the following lists of subjects would you most like to study?

❑ **1.** Biology, botany, chemistry, ecology, horticulture, zoology.

❑ **2.** Art, computer-aided design, drafting, construction trades, geometry.

❑ **3.** Art, broadcasting, creative writing, graphic design, journalism, music, theater arts.

❑ **4.** Accounting, business, cooperative education, economics, information technology.

❑ **5.** Child development, family and consumer studies, psychology, social studies, sociology.

❑ **6.** Accounting, business law, business math, economics, personal finance.

❑ **7.** Civics and government, current events, debate, foreign language, history, philosophy.

❑ **8.** Biology, chemistry, health, math, occupational health, language arts.

❑ **9.** Culinary arts, food service, foreign language, geography, language arts, speech.

❑ **10.** Anthropology, family and consumer science, foreign language, language arts, psychology, sociology.

❑ **11.** Communication, computer applications, graphic design, math, science, technology education.

❑ **12.** First aid, forensic science, government, health, history, language arts, law enforcement, psychology.

❑ **13.** Chemistry, geometry, language arts, physics, shop, trades.

- ❑ 14. Business education, computer applications, distributive education, economics, language arts, marketing.
- ❑ 15. Computer-aided design, computer networking, drafting, electronics, engineering, math, science.
- ❑ 16. Economics, foreign language, math, physical science, trade and industry.

Which type of afterschool club or activity are you more likely to join?

- ❑ 1. 4-H, Future Farmers of America (FFA), community gardening.
- ❑ 2. Habitat for Humanity, construction club, trade apprenticeship.
- ❑ 3. Dance, drama, chorus, marching band, newspaper staff, yearbook staff.
- ❑ 4. Future Business Leaders of America (FBLA), Junior Achievement.
- ❑ 5. National Honor Society, peer-to-peer mentor, tutor.
- ❑ 6. Stock Market Game, investment club.
- ❑ 7. Student government, debate team.
- ❑ 8. Sports trainer, Health Occupations Students of America (HOSA), Red Cross volunteer.
- ❑ 9. Culture Club, International Club, Model United Nations Club.
- ❑ 10. Beta Club; Key Club; Family, Career and Community Leaders of America (FCCLA).
- ❑ 11. High-Tech Club, Technology Student Association (TSA), Video Gamers Club.
- ❑ 12. Law Enforcement Explorer Post.
- ❑ 13. Odyssey of the Mind, SkillsUSA/Vocational Industrial Clubs of America (VICA).
- ❑ 14. Distributive Education Clubs of America (DECA) Marketing Club, junior fashion advisory board.

☐ **15.** Junior Engineering Technical Society (JETS), math club, National High School Science Bowl, science club.

☐ **16.** Environmental awareness clubs, National High School Solar Car Race.

Which of the following weekend activities would you most enjoy doing?

☐ **1.** Fishing, hunting, or hiking.

☐ **2.** Building a house for a needy family with Habitat for Humanity.

☐ **3.** Going to a concert or to see the latest movie.

☐ **4.** Getting a part-time job.

☐ **5.** Volunteering at the library or reading stories to children at a homeless shelter.

☐ **6.** Staying up all night playing Monopoly with friends.

☐ **7.** Working on a favorite political candidate's election campaign.

☐ **8.** Hosting a big birthday bash for a friend.

☐ **9.** Helping out at the local Ronald McDonald House or children's hospital.

☐ **10.** Taking a Red Cross first aid course or disaster-relief course.

☐ **11.** Playing a new video game or setting up a new home page for social networking.

☐ **12.** Watching all your favorite cop shows on TV.

☐ **13.** Giving your room an eco-makeover.

☐ **14.** Making posters to celebrate homecoming or a big school event.

☐ **15.** Competing in a local science fair.

☐ **16.** Building a soapbox derby car to race with friends.

Which of the following group of words best describes you?

- ❏ 1. Adventurous, eco-friendly, outdoorsy, physically active.
- ❏ 2. Artistic, curious, detail oriented, patient, persistent, visual thinker.
- ❏ 3. Creative, determined, dramatic, imaginative, talkative, tenacious.
- ❏ 4. Logical, natural leader, practical, organized, responsible, tactful.
- ❏ 5. Attentive, decisive, friendly, helpful, innovative, inquisitive.
- ❏ 6. Efficient, good with numbers, logical, methodical, orderly, self-confident, trustworthy.
- ❏ 7. Articulate, competitive, organized, persuasive, problem-solver, service minded.
- ❏ 8. Attentive, careful, caring, compassionate, conscientious, patient, task oriented.
- ❏ 9. Adventurous, easygoing, fun loving, outgoing, self-motivated, tactful.
- ❏ 10. Accepting, attentive, articulate, intuitive, logical, sensible, thrifty.
- ❏ 11. Accurate, analytical, detail oriented, focused, logical, persistent, precise, technology whiz.
- ❏ 12. Adventurous, community minded, courageous, dependable, decisive, fair, optimistic.
- ❏ 13. Active, coordinated, inquisitive, observant, practical, steady.
- ❏ 14. Competitive, creative, enthusiastic, persuasive, self-motivated.
- ❏ 15. Curious about how things work, detail oriented, inquisitive, objective, mechanically inclined, observant.
- ❏ 16. Coordinated, mechanical, multitasker, observant, prepared, realistic.

If you could do only one thing to make the world a better place, which of the following would you do?

☐   **1.**   Eliminate hunger everywhere.

☐   **2.**   Create sustainable, eco-friendly environments.

☐   **3.**   Keep the world entertained and informed.

☐   **4.**   Provide meaningful jobs and fair trade opportunities for everyone.

☐   **5.**   Teach the world to read so that no one is limited by a lack of education.

☐   **6.**   Keep national and global financial systems on track.

☐   **7.**   Promote world peace and stable governments for all.

☐   **8.**   Provide access to high-quality health care services for everyone.

☐   **9.**   Bridge cultural differences through communication and collaboration.

☐   **10.**   Help people in need get back on their feet.

☐   **11.**   Use technology to solve the world's most pressing problems.

☐   **12.**   Make the world a safer place where justice prevails.

☐   **13.**   Discover a new innovation on par with Edison's invention of electricity that has the potential to improve the quality of life for all mankind.

☐   **14.**   Get the word out about a favorite issue or cause.

☐   **15.**   Find a cure for cancer, AIDS, or other life-threatening disease.

☐   **16.**   Develop more efficient ways to get people and things where they need to go.

Which of the following lists of career options intrigues you most?

❑ **1.** Agricultural economist, botanist, food broker, food scientist, forester, geologist, hydrologist, nutritionist, recycler, wastewater manager.

❑ **2.** Civil engineer, demolition technician, energy-efficient builder, heavy-equipment operator, landscape architect, urban planner.

❑ **3.** Actor, blogger, commercial artist, digital media specialist, museum curator, social medial consultant, stage manager, writer.

❑ **4.** Advertising account executive, brand manager, budget analyst, chief executive officer, dispatcher, e-commerce analyst, green entrepreneur, international businessperson, purchasing agent.

❑ **5.** Animal trainer, coach, college professor, corporate trainer, guidance counselor, principal, speech pathologist, textbook publisher.

❑ **6.** Accountant, banker, chief financial officer, economist, fraud investigator, investment adviser, property manager, stock broker, wealth manager.

❑ **7.** Bank examiner, city planner, customs agent, federal special agent, intelligence analyst, politician, private investigator.

❑ **8.** Art therapist, audiologist, chiropractor, dentist, massage therapist, pharmacist, surgeon, veterinarian.

❑ **9.** Banquet manager, chef, cruise ship captain, exhibit designer, golf pro, resort manager, theme park designer, tour guide, wedding planner.

❑ **10.** Career coach, child care director, elder care center manager, hairstylist, personal trainer, psychologist, religious leader, teacher, victim advocate.

❏ 11. Artificial intelligence scientist, chief information officer, computer forensics investigator, database modeler, e-commerce entrepreneur, Webmaster.

❏ 12. Animal control officer, coroner, detective, emergency medical technician, firefighter, lawyer, park ranger, warden, wildlife conservation officer.

❏ 13. Chemical engineer, hybrid car designer, industrial designer, logistician, millwright, nanotechnologist, robotics technologist, traffic engineer, welder.

❏ 14. Art designer, business development manager, copywriter, creative director, graphic designer, market researcher, media buyer, new media specialist, retail store manager, social media consultant.

❏ 15. Aeronautical engineer, anthropologist, chemist, ecologist, telecommunications engineer, mathematician, oceanographer, zoologist.

❏ 16. Air traffic controller, cargo inspector, flight attendant, logistics planner, pilot, railroad engineer, surveyor, truck driver.

Which of the following types of work environments would you most like to work in?

❏ 1. Farm, food processing plant, food science laboratory, forest, garden center, greenhouse, national park, recycling center.

❏ 2. Construction site, commercial facilities, government agency, corporate office, private firm, residential properties.

❏ 3. Independent, creative business, museum, news agency, publishing company, studio, theater.

❏ 4. Business planning office, corporate headquarters, government agency, international business center.

❑ 5. College counseling center, elementary school, high school, middle school, museum, preschool, school district office.

❑ 6. Accounting firm, bank, brokerage firm, corporate office, insurance company, stock market.

❑ 7. Business development office, chamber of commerce, city/county/state/federal government agency; courthouse; law firm.

❑ 8. Dental office, hospital, medical research center, pharmacy, physician's office, surgical complex, urgent care center, veterinary clinic.

❑ 9. Airport, amusement park, hotel, public park, resort, restaurant, sports center, travel agency, zoo.

❑ 10. Employment agency, consumer credit bureau, elder care center, fitness center, mental health care center, real estate office, school, spa.

❑ 11. Corporation, information technology company, new media development center, research and development laboratory, small business.

❑ 12. Courthouse, prison, fire station, government agency, law firm, national park, police station.

❑ 13. Manufacturing plant, design firm, engineering company, production facility, research and development laboratory.

❑ 14. Advertising agency, independent creative business, corporate marketing department, retail store, new media development center.

❑ 15. Science laboratory, engineering firm, information technology company, research and development center.

❑ 16. Airport, marina, mass transit authority, railroad, shipping port, subway system, transportation center.

Go back through your answers and record how many of each of the following numbers you have marked.

1s	2s	3s	4s	5s	6s	7s	8s
9s	10s	11s	12s	13s	14s	15s	16s

Discovery #7: My Interests and Skills...

What do your answers say about your personal preferences, natural inclinations, and ambitions? In what ways can you use these clues to better inform your career choices? What general direction are your skills and interests pointing toward? Describe below.

_____

_____

_____

_____

_____

_____

DISCOVER #8: WHICH CAREER PATH IS RIGHT FOR ME?

If you had more...	Consider this career cluster...	To explore careers that involve...
1s	Agriculture, Food, and Natural Resources	Producing, processing, marketing, distributing, financing, and developing agricultural commodities and resources including food, fiber, wood products, natural resources, horticulture, and other plant and animal products and resources.
2s	Architecture and Construction	Designing, planning, managing, building, and maintaining the built environment.
3s	Arts, A/V Technology, and Communications	Designing, producing, exhibiting, performing, writing, and publishing multimedia content including visual and performing arts and design, journalism, and entertainment services.
4s	Business, Management, and Administration	Planning, organizing, directing, and evaluating business functions essential to efficient and productive business operations.
5s	Education and Training	Planning, managing, and providing education and training services, and related learning support services.
6s	Finance	Planning services for financial and investment planning, banking, insurance, and business financial management.
7s	Government and Public Service	Governing, planning, regulating, managing, and administering governmental functions at the local, state, and federal levels.
8s	Health Science	Planning, managing, and providing therapeutic services, diagnostic services, health informatics, support services, and biotechnology research and development.

(continues)

(continued)

If you had more...	Consider this career cluster...	To explore careers that involve...
9s	Hospitality and Tourism	Managing, marketing, and operating restaurants and other food services, lodging, attractions, recreation events, and travel-related services.
10s	Human Services	Preparing individuals for employment in career pathways that relate to families and human needs.
11s	Information Technology	Designing, developing, supporting, and managing hardware, software, multimedia, and systems integration services.
12s	Law, Public Safety, Corrections, and Security	Planning, managing, and providing legal, public safety, protective services, and homeland security, including professional and technical support services.
13s	Manufacturing	Planning, managing, and performing the processing of materials into intermediate or final products and related professional and technical support activities.
14s	Marketing	Planning, managing, and performing marketing activities to reach organizational objectives.
15s	Science, Technology, Engineering, and Mathematics	Planning, managing, and providing scientific research and professional and technical services including laboratory and testing services, and research and development services.
16s	Transportation, Distribution, and Logistics	Planning, managing, and moving people, materials, and goods by road, pipeline, air, rail, and water, and related professional and technical support services.

Gratefully adapted and used with permission from the States' Career Clusters Initiative.

Discovery #8: My Career Path

With all scores tallied and all interests considered, where should you begin exploring your future career? List the three career clusters you most want to explore here:

1 _____

2 _____

3 _____

As you can probably guess, each title in the *Career Ideas for Teens* series is based on one of the career clusters described above. For the most effective career exploration process, start with the title most in sync with both your assessment results and your gut instincts about what you want to do with your life.

No matter which title you choose, be prepared to encounter exciting opportunities you've never considered—maybe even some you've never heard of before. You may find that your interests, skills, and ambitions lead you to a specific career idea that inspires your immediate plans for the future. On the other hand, those same interests, skills, and ambitions may simply point you toward a particular pathway or industry segment such as agriculture or education. That's just fine, too. Time, experience, opportunities— and the "Experiment with Success" activities you'll encounter in Section Three—will eventually converge to get you right where you want to be.

YOU ARE
HERE

If you scored high in and are especially curious about...	Start exploring career options in Section Two of...
Agriculture, Food, and Natural Resources	*Career Ideas for Teens in Agriculture, Food, and Natural Resources*
Architecture and Construction	*Career Ideas for Teens in Architecture and Construction, Second Edition*
Arts, A/V Technology, and Communications	*Career Ideas for Teens in the Arts and Communications, Second Edition*
Business, Management, and Administration	*Career Ideas for Teens in Business, Management, and Administration*
Education and Training	*Career Ideas for Teens in Education and Training, Second Edition*
Finance	*Career Ideas for Teens in Finance*
Government and Public Service	*Career Ideas for Teens in Government and Public Service, Second Edition*
Health Science	*Career Ideas for Teens in Health Science, Second Edition*
Hospitality and Tourism	*Career Ideas for Teens in Hospitality and Tourism*
Human Services	*Career Ideas for Teens in Human Services*
Information Technology	*Career Ideas for Teens in Information Technology, Second Edition*
Law, Public Safety, Corrections, and Security	*Career Ideas for Teens in Law and Public Safety, Second Edition*
Manufacturing	*Career Ideas for Teens in Manufacturing, Second Edition*
Marketing	*Career Ideas for Teens in Marketing*
Science, Technology, Engineering, and Mathematics	*Career Ideas for Teens in Science, Technology, Engineering, and Math*
Transportation, Distribution, and Logistics	*Career Ideas for Teens in Transportation, Distribution, and Logistics*

DISCOVER #9: CAREER RÉSUMÉ

In "Me, Myself, and I," you summarized all your discoveries in a "me" résumé. This time, shift the focus to create a career résumé that describes what you currently consider a "dream job." Use a blend of your own wants and opportunities you'd expect to find along your favorite career path to fill in the categories below.

Career Title _____

_____

Job Description _____

_____

_____

Skills Needed _____

_____

_____

Knowledge Required _____

_____

_____

Work Environment _____

_____

_____

Perks and Benefits _____

_____

_____

MOVING ON

Ready to start exploring career ideas? Section Two is where potential and possibilities meet. As you start exploring options associated with this career path, look for those careers that best match the discoveries you've made about yourself. Make sure any opportunity you decide to pursue matches up with all you've just learned about your ambitions, skills, interests, values, and work style.

EXPLORE YOUR OPTIONS

If you are reading this book, chances are you have a teacher to thank. Somewhere down the line someone (more likely, many someones) made the decision to devote their lives to teaching students like you, and you are smarter, more educated, and better prepared for the future because of it.

Perhaps, you are considering becoming a teacher yourself someday. If that's the case your potential workplace options include child care centers, schools, colleges and universities, corporate offices, and other places where teaching and learning occur on a regular basis.

The success of every industry and profession you can imagine hinges upon the success of education and training. Think about it: Without educators and trainers, there would be no doctors, no engineers, and no lawyers. Without the efforts of educators and other trainers, workers in every profession would lack even the basic skills necessary to read, write, and function in civilized society.

When you think of careers in education and training, the first job title that pops into your head is probably "teacher." And, of course, teachers are a big part of the education and training "industry." Meeting the needs of millions of learners every year, however, requires the services of a wide variety of professionals who plan, develop, manage, and provide actual education and training services as well as the support services that make learning possible.

In the following section, you'll find in-depth profiles of 35 careers related in one way or another to education. As you explore these (and other) careers, you may notice that some careers are more alike than others. The careers that have a lot in common can be grouped into different "pathways." Understanding these pathways provides another important clue about which direction might be best for you. The three education and training pathways include:

TEACHING AND TRAINING

According to experts associated with the U.S. Department of Education's Career Clusters Initiative, there are excellent opportunities ahead for people who choose to pursue careers in teaching and training. A huge demand is expected for well-educated professionals with the ability to effectively communicate their knowledge in a given subject to people of all ages. Many occupations in this field require licensing or certification, in addition to postsecondary credentials that range from the associate's degrees in child development required for many child care workers to the doctorates required for college professors.

Training and education careers include career and technical education instructor, coach, college and university professor, cooperative extension agent, corporate trainer, elementary teacher, English as a Second Language (ESL) instructor, environmental educator, fitness trainer, museum educator, paraprofessional, physical education teacher, public health educator, secondary school teacher, and special education teacher.

PROFESSIONAL SUPPORT SERVICES

The professional support pathway represents a wide variety of highly specialized professions that enhance and sustain the education system. This pathway includes those professions that assist people with personal and family needs, mental health problems, educational goals, and career decision making. Most of the work conducted by these professionals takes place outside of classrooms and their services are often provided to individuals and families as opposed to groups of students.

Careers in this pathway include audiologist, career counselor, guidance counselor, school psychologist, and school social worker.

ADMINISTRATION AND ADMINISTRATIVE SUPPORT

Keeping educational programs and facilities running smoothly is the number one priority of administration and administrative support personnel. Administrators provide the direction, leadership, and management that make for effective learning environments at every level, whether it's a preschool, university, correctional facility, or job-training organization.

Education attorney and advocate, instructional coordinator, principal, and student affairs officer are examples of administration and administrative support professions.

A NOTE ON WEB SITES
Web sites tend to move around a bit. If you have trouble finding a specific site referred to in the following career profiles, use a favorite search engine to search for a specific Web site or type of information.

As you explore the individual careers in this book and others in this series, remember to keep what you've learned about yourself in mind. Consider each option in light of what you know about your interests, strengths, work values, and work personality.

Pay close attention to the job requirements. Is math aptitude needed? Good writing skills? Ability to take things apart and visualize how they go back together? If you don't have the necessary abilities (or don't have a strong desire to acquire them), you probably won't enjoy the job.

For instance, enriching young minds may sound like a noble profession, and it is. However, when considering whether teaching is right for you, think about the realities of being in a classroom with children or adults all day—every day, week after week, and year after year. For some people this is an exciting and fulfilling prospect. If this is the case for you, be sure to explore every available opportunity to teach or train until you find just the right place to share your skills and expertise.

For those who suspect they might not flourish in a situation involving daily involvement with rooms full of people—young or old—there are other options. If preparing others for productive futures is an important value that you absolutely want to incorporate into your vocation, be open to some of the very interesting options associated with administration or professional support.

Adult Literacy Teacher

Imagine that you have never learned to read. You can spot a few words here and there, but you cannot pick up a newspaper and understand the headlines, nor can you fill out a job application properly. You can't read a map to find your way to another town. You can't balance your checkbook. You can't even read the books your seven-year-old brings home from the library. In many ways, you are shut out of the world. Many adults are in this situation, but adult literacy teachers are hard at work to give them the gift of literacy.

For a variety of reasons some students never finish their schooling and do not become proficient readers. An adult literacy teacher develops classes that help adults learn to read and write, and sometimes learn other subjects. Some adult learners just want to improve their reading and writing to a level of basic competency, but many want to get a General Equivalency Diploma, or GED, which is the equivalent of a high school diploma. A GED can be the difference between being unemployed and getting a job.

As with elementary and secondary education, different states follow different curriculum standards. By the time adult literacy students complete a reading program, they should have sufficient

CAREER 411

Search It!
The Commission on Adult Basic Education at http://www.coabe.org/index.cfm and the Association of Adult Literacy Professional Developers at http://www.aalpd.org.

Surf It!
Play games on the National Adult Literacy Agency Web site at http://www.literacytools.ie/games.cfm.

Read It!
The Adult Education Content Standards Warehouse (http://www.adultedcontentstandards.ed.gov/Source/GetStandard.asp) contains an index and links for state standards for adult literacy instruction.

Learn It!
Minimum Education: Bachelor's degree, some states require additional teaching certification.

Typical Majors: Teaching, math, English, early childhood education, psychology.

Special Skills: Excellent communication and leadership skills, organizational skills, ability to teach others, patience, flexibility, good reading and writing skills, assessment skills, acceptance of students' diversity.

Earn It!
Median annual salary is $45,920.
(Source: U.S. Department of Labor)

GET STARTED NOW!

- In School: English, writing, psychology, personal finance, life skills, and career-based classes. Foreign language classes, especially Spanish, will help you work with second-language speakers.
- After School: Volunteer to tutor adults in literacy or to read to young children.
- Around Town: Visit the main branch of your public library. Many libraries provide adult literacy support and are always in need of volunteers.

knowledge of phonemic awareness (the ability to understand spoken words) and phonics, vocabulary and word choice, sentence structure, comprehension, an understanding of different writing genres, and basic writing skills. Students should also, according to some standards, be able to use reference materials; read dates, times, and handwriting; and fill out forms. Some states require certification to teach adult literacy, and teachers may be required to follow their state's standards in the same way as all other teachers.

In many ways, teaching adult literacy is like teaching any other class. Teachers must prepare lesson plans based on students' needs, assign and grade work, and prepare students for tests. Teachers also need to tailor their lessons to students' interests. For example, a teacher might use picture books with adult students who have children, since those adults can then share the picture books at home. Adults have commitments, however, that sometimes interfere with their schooling. Work, sick children, and other issues may prevent some students from attending class regularly. Likewise, many adults who need remediation or literacy training have disabilities or other challenges that prevented them from completing their education, and these issues may still be present into adulthood.

IF YOU WERE. . .

As an adult literacy teacher, how would you teach your students to fill out job applications?

. . . MAKE IT REAL!

Go online to find samples of simple job applications. Think of ways to introduce the concept to adult learners and create an interesting lesson plan. For extra authenticity, make a video of yourself teaching the lesson, explaining the process line by line and step by step. Watch the video as if you were one of your future students. Would you learn how to fill out a job application?

Adult literacy teaching positions are often limited to part-time hours. Teaching facilities for adults may lack modern technology and other amenities, which is why they often take place in recreation centers, churches, and other "volunteer" buildings. Fortunately adult students are usually eager to learn and highly motivated, and are truly thankful for their teachers.

Animal Trainer

Look at your dog. He is asleep on his cushion, snoring away, but he could have had a different life. With a little training, he could have been a therapy dog, a service animal, a performer, or even a police dog. People who love animals can train them to do almost anything.

Animals enrich our lives just by their presence, but animal trainers teach "working animals" to perform specialized tasks. Basic obedience trainers can work freelance or in pet stores. The job starts with teaching people's pets to behave, and to respond to commands like "Heel" and "Stay." Trainers can also teach especially calm pets to be therapy animals. For example, quiet dogs make great listeners for children who are learning to read. Animal visits make hospital and nursing home stays more tolerable. Animal trainers work patiently with animals and owners to provide consistent instruction; the animal must know what you want, and consistently receive praise and rewards for correct responses.

Can you imagine *Harry Potter* films without Hedwig the owl, or *Lassie* reruns without Lassie? Animals add an extra dimension

GET STARTED NOW!

- In School: All the basics plus leadership, first aid, personal training.
- After School: Volunteer at the zoo, a vet's office or shelter, or work at a pet store to get as much experience with different animals as possible.
- Around Town: Ask to interview a K-9 unit officer at your local police department. Meet with the officer and his dog so you can observe the relationship firsthand, and ask questions about how the animal is trained, how he behaves on and off duty, etc.

to movies, television and stage shows, and commercials. Studio animal trainers' goals are the same for any animal from a puppy to an elephant—to modify the animal's behavior and to help it learn numerous tasks. The trainers ensure that the animals are well cared for and that they perform consistently. (Some zoo animals receive training in order to make them easier to care for, too.) Studio animal trainers work long hours, crouch in uncomfortable positions to stay out of camera range, and do heavy lifting and other labor, like poop scooping. And remember—animals need the same care on weekends and holidays. This career is a lifestyle, not just a job!

Service animal trainers teach animals to perform essential tasks that humans cannot perform easily. For example, service dogs assist the blind when navigating streets and stairs. Animals alert hearing-impaired people to ringing phones and doorbells. People with limited mobility gain balance and steadiness from canine companions, while a person in a wheelchair can use a monkey helper to retrieve objects. Some trainers even teach animals to alert owners at the onset of seizures. Other trainers teach service animals to sniff out drugs, bombs, and customs contraband. Perhaps the most familiar service animals are the loyal dogs (often German shepherd dogs) that ride with their police partner, and bloodhounds that search for lost people.

IF YOU WERE. . .

As an animal trainer preparing a dog to perform in agility events, what tricks would you teach a dog?

. . . MAKE IT REAL!

Visit the United States Dog Agility Association's Web site (http://www.usdaa.com) and read this article on the Agility Ability Web site at http://www.agilityability.com/agility_training.htm. Watch some agility tricks on YouTube (http://www.youtube.com/watch?v=RWb2cYyMS6k). Then, draw a dog agility course and create "paw prints" to show how the dog should run through it.

Animal trainers must be patient, consistent, and kind to win animals' trust. An animal trainer must properly care for animals, including administering medicine and keeping health and performance records. They should be able to easily spot animals that are good candidates for training and service. Most importantly, when an animal's work is done, trainers match their special friend to a loving, caring owner.

Career Counselor

You are the high school's lead career counselor. Today is the job fair, which you have organized. You contacted local and national companies and asked them to send representatives, and they are arriving in droves, but you are not worried. You have coached your high school seniors on how to dress professionally, how to ask intelligent questions, and how to create career portfolios. They know they need good SAT and ACT scores to get into colleges that will help move them forward in these careers. You are so proud of them and cannot wait to see them interact with the professionals who will one day be hiring them.

Career counselors work with high school and college students who need advice about what they should be doing to ensure they get on the career paths they want. Career counselors also work with people in the workforce, who often change careers for different reasons. Sometimes the careers are a bad match for workers' abilities. Or, the income, typical working hours, or prospects for advancement do not match workers' goals. Sometimes seasoned employees with a lot of experience realize they are burned out and want new challenges. A career counselor helps all of these people change their careers and their lives.

GET STARTED NOW!

- In School: Psychology and counseling, communications classes, writing classes, business.
- After School: Interview your school guidance counselor and find out what she does to counsel students about future careers. Ask her to refer you to any resources that are useful for choosing a career.
- Around Town: Volunteer to help organize a career-day event at your own school or a local elementary school.

CAREER 411

Search It!
The National Career Development Association at http://associationdatabase.com/aws/NCDA/pt/sp/home_page.

Surf It!
Try a color test that claims to identify good career paths according to color preferences at the Dewey Color System Web site: http://deweycolorsystem.com/personality-test. Click "Take the Test" to get started.

Read It!
Check out Monster's career management tools at http://my.monster.com/Career-Management/Landing.aspx.

Learn It!
Minimum Education: Bachelor's degree, some school-based jobs will require a master's degree.

Typical Majors: Counseling, psychology, communications, sociology, career education.

Special Skills: Excellent communication and listening skills, research skills, organizational skills, desire to help others, conflict resolution ability, discretion.

Earn It!
Median annual salary is $52,550.
(Source: U.S. Department of Labor)

Career counselors are similar to other types of counselors in that they work with clients to help them learn about themselves and teach them how to use that information to their advantage. A career counselor's primary job is to find occupational options that are a good fit for clients' interests, skills, and goals. This process often starts by guiding clients through a thorough self-assessment process. To do that, career counselors must listen closely to their clients and correctly administer tests, such as the Myers-Briggs personality test, and interpret results.

Career counselors also must know a lot about a wide variety of careers. They need specific knowledge of the many variations that occur within certain fields. For this reason, many successful career counselors leave other fields and then counsel those who want to work in those fields they left. For example, a head nurse in a hospital might become a career counselor who specialized in teaching nursing students about the different types of nursing.

IF YOU WERE. . .

As a career counselor, what career would you advise your best friend or close family member to pursue?

. . . MAKE IT REAL!

Choose a friend or family member and have them take the Myers-Briggs-type test at http://www.humanmetrics. com/cgi-win/JTypes2.asp. Check careers that apply to their results at http://www.personalitypage.com/careers. html. Next, ask your "client" to check off the transferable skills she thinks she has, from this list at http://www. quintcareers.com/transferable_skills_set.html. Write a report listing the results of the testing and your career recommendations.

Career counselors' services can include helping clients with job searches, résumé building, coaching them for interviews, and teaching networking and salary negotiation skills. With all of these skills available to clients, a person who uses a career counselor, while not guaranteed a job, should definitely be armed for a career, or a career change.

Coach

CAREER 411

Search It!

National High School Coaches Association at http://www.nhsca.com and National Collegiate Athletic Association at http://www.ncaa.org.

Surf It!

Go online to Be the Coach at http://www. bethecoachbasketball.com. Or visit the "Quiz the Coach" section of the Kidzworld Web site at http://www. kidzworld.com/advice/get-physical.

Read It!

Read some inspiring letters about 10 inspiring coaches at http://espn.go.com/page2/s/list/topcoaches/010518.html.

Learn It!

Minimum Education: Bachelor's degree and sports experience.

Typical Majors: Sports psychology, health studies, sports management.

Special Skills: Ability to communicate with a diverse population, integrity and honesty, flexibility, persistence, creativity, stress tolerance, and a strong desire to win.

Earn It!

Median annual salary is $28,380.

(Source: U.S. Department of Labor)

It's the bottom of the 9th inning and the score is tied 3–3. Your team has two outs, and the next batter is stepping up to the plate. This kid is a great hitter, but he has a tendency to rush things and not let the ball come to him. Strike one! Ugh, come on, kid. That was way too low to swing at. Ball one! That's better; make him pitch to you. Then, there it is—a high fastball, his favorite pitch. Kaboom! It's outta there! Whoops, you're soaked. You forgot about the Gatorade.

Remember your first sports experience? It may have been T-ball, soccer, basketball, field hockey, or something else. Or maybe you took tennis lessons, swimming lessons, cheerleading, or figure skating. Chances are, your first coach was the mom or dad of a teammate, or maybe it was one of your own parents, volunteering to help out. Back then you learned that coaches are responsible for helping players learn the skills, strategies, and rules of the game. You probably looked up to your coach with respect. At any level, a coach must act in a way so as to earn players' respect, and must also know the game inside and out.

High school coaches often teach classes, too. Along with conducting practices and running games, they also purchase equipment, schedule practices, advise athletes about nutrition and

GET STARTED NOW!

- In School: Play sports! Try to find one you really enjoy and stick with it.
- After School: Many sports offer out-of-school experiences over the summer. Check out team or club sports at your local recreation center.
- Around Town: Volunteer to work in children's sports. For example, umpire for T-ball or softball, coach soccer, or get your lifeguard's certificate and coach swimming.

training, and even fund-raise money for team travel and special equipment. Coaches usually work with team sports within a high school, but can work with competitors in individual sports as well.

College coaching is highly specialized; these coaches are trained professionals who often played the sport themselves. In addition to conducting team practices and running games, they usually supervise a staff of scouts, specialized assistant coaches, and equipment managers. For some sports and in some programs, coaches endure a lot of pressure to win, and therefore command high salaries. They must attract top-notch players with scholarships, maintain absolute adherence to NCAA rules, and win regular- and post-season games. These coaches also supervise a staff that allocates money for scholarships and travel, arranges team meals and travel accommodations, and governs special team housing, in some cases. Coaches also often make appearances at alumni and charity events to help raise money for causes or for the university.

Good coaches easily communicate with players and parents. They must keep up with administrative requirements. They must be experts in their sports, and they must be able to choose the best

IF YOU WERE. . .

As a peewee T-ball coach, how would you introduce your young player to the basics of the game?

. . . MAKE IT REAL!

Go online to research the rules of the game. Create a set of T-ball rule trading cards that visually explain how the game is played. Keep the rules simple and specific.

players and bring out their best possible performances. But above all else, a coach must set a good example. The skills you teach players on the field or in the gym, like teamwork, perseverance, and determination, are important in everyday life, too.

College Dean

"Dean" is the title given to the person who oversees a college or school within a university. There are deans of schools of medicine, deans of colleges of arts and sciences, and many more. Deans' responsibilities vary widely, but here are some common job functions.

First, an academic dean supervises assistant and associate deans and department chairs. Since deans are promoted from within a department, they must demonstrate leadership and integrity as professors. The dean hires, evaluates, and mentors faculty; determines salaries; and assigns tenure. (A tenured professor cannot be fired without just cause and due process.) Deans and assistants also govern academic integrity for the college. An assistant dean might approve departmental Web site content and press releases, and sign off on academic paperwork on behalf of the dean's office.

An academic dean is also in charge of guiding the college's future. The dean works with assistant and associate deans and department chairs to plan for recruiting and hiring faculty; allocating and managing operating funds (including research grant

CAREER 411

Search It!
Association of Deans and Directors of University Colleges and Undergraduate Studies at http://adandd.org.

Surf It!
Dean Dad is a blogger who also happens to be a dean at a community college: http://www.insidehighered.com/blogs/confessions_of_a_community_college_dean.

Read It!
Read "So You Want to Be a Dean?" on the *Chronicle of Higher Education* Web site at http://chronicle.com/article/So-You-Want-to-Be-a-Dean-/46065.

Learn It!
Minimum Education: Doctoral degree.

Typical Majors: Any major—universities have deans for each major such as science, medicine, and engineering among others.

Special Skills: Leadership skills, integrity, diligence, desire to help people, excellent communication and listening skills, problem-solving skills, persistence, attention to detail.

Earn It!
Median annual salary is $82,800.
(Source: U.S. Department of Labor)

GET STARTED NOW!

- In School: College prep, plus writing and communications.
- After School: Seek out leadership positions for school projects and clubs. Be a good leader and treat your classmates like colleagues. Respect their ideas and work as a team. Also, improve your writing and speaking skills.
- Around Town: Volunteer for a leadership position in the community. Ask what help is needed at charity organizations, your place of worship, or at a local recreation center. Practice working well with the adults who oversee organizing the event.

monies), procuring more building space, equipment, and renovations; and developing and overseeing interdisciplinary programs. (For example, a major in something like Asian studies might require classes in literature, geography, sociology, and other disciplines.)

Here are two examples of planning. First, as dean of a college of education, you might anticipate that most of your department will retire within six years. You would be responsible for planning to recruit and promote replacement faculty or reallocate responsibilities to remaining faculty in time to meet the demand as colleagues retire. As the dean of a school of dentistry, you dislike turning away highly qualified students because the school's facility is at capacity, so you would create a plan for acquiring space on campus to build a new dentistry building, and then raise building funds through gifting and grants.

This leads to another function of a dean: fund-raising. Since deans allocate resources to different departments, they know what funds are needed. Appearing at fund-raising events, sitting on community boards and committees, and advocating for funding allocation through the school administration are all important facets of a dean's job. Representing a school at these types of functions makes a dean's job very political; tact is a good quality for a dean.

Most professors do not set out to become deans. The university provost taps exceptional faculty who have shown talent as department chairs. Being a dean still means giving back to students by making sure all of their college experiences are worthwhile and the faculty members who teach them are excellent.

College Professor

CAREER 411

Search It!
American Association of University Professors at www.aaup.org and Association of American Colleges and Universities at http://www.aacu.org.

Surf It!
The social networking site RateMyProfessors.com: http://www.ratemyprofessors.com.

Read It!
Read blogs from a wide variety of professors at http://www.onlinecollege.org/2009/10/12/100-best-professors-who-blog.

Learn It!
Minimum Education: Doctoral degree for tenured faculty; master's degree for associate professor opportunities; master's or bachelor's degree for community college professors.

Typical Majors: Subject of interest.

Special Skills: Perseverance, patience, leadership, excellent listening and communication skills, time management skills, research skills, and public speaking skills.

Earn It!
Median annual salary is $58,830.

(Source: U.S. Department of Labor)

You have graded your undergraduates' tests, reviewed three journal articles, and are off to meet with the graduate admissions committee. Tonight you will complete the chapter you are contributing to a colleague's book, then prepare for Wednesday's night class. It's good that you love your job, since you do it around the clock.

Teaching at the postsecondary level is different from teaching in high school. Classes range from giant lectures with hundreds of students, to tiny seminars with fewer than 10 students, to one student working with a teacher on an independent study. Professors even create and manage online courses, for which they must develop course work, assign and grade projects and papers, and determine students' grades. Professors also spend a lot of time advising master's degree and doctoral students. But there is much more to being a college professor than teaching and advising.

College professors are experts in their fields. They keep up with the latest developments in their areas of expertise, and they

GET STARTED NOW!

- In School: Focus on a field that interests you and study as much as you can in that subject. Also pursue opportunities to hone your speaking and writing skills.
- After School: Research two universities and compare their course offerings in your interest area. Look at faculty size and degrees offered.
- Around Town: Visit a local vocational school, college, or university campus. If possible, schedule an interview with a professor and ask questions about the job.

also forge these developments. At top research universities a large portion of a professor's time is devoted to reading journal articles, performing field research or experiments, gathering and analyzing data, and then publishing their own work in professional journals or books. At many schools it's "publish or perish"; professors have to publish a continuous and significant stream of articles and research in order to achieve tenure—a lifetime appointment often granted to professors after sufficient exemplary work and publications—and several years of service to the school. A professor with tenure cannot be fired without just cause and due process. (While vocational and technical instructors may not teach at universities that offer tenure, they must still keep up with technological advancements and other changes in their fields.)

Besides teaching, research, and publishing, professors perform services for the school and for relevant organizations. Many professors help determine book and grant awards, and serve on committees to select candidates for advanced degree programs. Professors also read and comment on journal articles and serve on journal editorial boards. There is no additional pay for this work, but it is crucial for a professor who wants to achieve tenure.

Becoming a professor takes many years. You have to plan your educational funding carefully, since pay is often low at first. A professor's schedule is flexible, but there is often no clear line between work time and playtime. The work becomes a leisure pastime as well as a job. If you are fortunate enough to find an interest that you love enough to study, write about, and debate all the time, you can become a respected teacher and expert in your field.

Cooperative Extension Agent

You're heading to the community college to lead the baby clothes sewing group. Today's lesson: adding snaps. You will also present the county gardening awards to the 4-H group. Next you return phone calls from people with questions like, "My power went off three hours ago. Is the food in my refrigerator still safe to eat?" and, "What do I do about the skunk under my house?" You help a visitor who brings in canned goods she thinks have spoiled. (She's right!) In your spare time you keep bees, so tonight you will give a PowerPoint presentation showing farmers how to run beekeeping facilities. This is all part of the daily roller coaster that is the job of a cooperative extension agent.

Cooperative extension agencies are the educational outreach arm of NIFA, the National Institute of Food and Agriculture. NIFA was started to help make the educational resources of agricultural and technical universities, sometimes called land-grant universities, accessible to the public Extension agencies sponsor public programs, field all kinds of strange and interesting questions, and share their knowledge about innovations in science,

GET STARTED NOW!

- In School: Horticulture, agriculture, personal finance, family consumer science (home economics), biology, math, psychology, writing classes.
- After School: Join or volunteer for 4-H (http://www.4-h.org) to get firsthand experience with the organization.
- Around Town: Consider working in a community garden or volunteering at a farm.

agriculture, and engineering. NIFA has broadened its focus to provide services to urban and suburban populations. Agents usually serve the population within a designated territory, such as a county or parish.

There are four basic categories of extension agents. One category provides agricultural information: improved farming and ranching methods, care of livestock, cultivating and harvesting crops, and financing for farms. Another category specializes in family consumer science, and employs experts on home management practices like budgeting, raising children, and nutrition and meal preparation. A third category employs agents who work with youth, often through the 4-H program (the youth education branch of cooperative extension). The final category of agents deals with environmental concerns in urban and rural settings. Extension agents' expertise and areas of personal interest determine the categories they fulfill.

Cooperative extension agencies still educate farmers about agricultural innovations. Outside organizations, such as churches or volunteer groups, may invite extension agencies to provide information and services for their members. Extension agents also work one-on-one with individuals who have questions or problems. Extension agencies rely on referrals to gather clients, but they also market their services to the community by advertising programs like the beekeeping presentation, holding contests like the county gardening contest for 4-H members, and sponsoring group learning experiences like the sewing class.

Candidates for this position should have a desire to help people from all walks of life. They should also expect to be "interruption driven," which means dropping what they are doing to answer questions. This job offers fieldwork, variety, and some night and weekend hours, since that is when most people have time to attend programs. While there is office work involved in preparing presentations and doing research, you will not find much time to sit still.

Corporate Trainer

New employees have a lot to learn at SafetyFirst Security. They need to learn how to use the phone and computer systems, as well as how to install and operate security equipment. They need customer service training. Certain employees require training in surveillance and risk assessment so that nobody gets hurt. Former police officers need training for transitioning to the civilian arena, since security is a different ball game than law enforcement. When anything changes, everyone needs to be retrained—again. It is your job to ensure that your company's employees keep their clients—and themselves—as safe as possible.

Just as teachers teach students, corporate trainers train employees. They provide learning experiences designed to help employees work smarter. There's nothing new about the fact that many companies have training sessions for both new and seasoned employees, but the rapid changes that take place in certain areas have created a need for exclusively dedicated trainers.

Technology is one of these rapidly changing areas. Since, for example, you do not want the marketing manager to spend an entire morning reading the operating manual for the new phone system, or days struggling with a new software package, a corporate trainer could plan demonstration sessions for employees. It's important for employees to spend as little time as possible learn-

GET STARTED NOW!

- In School: College prep, plus public speaking and communications.
- After School: Volunteer to be a peer mediator or tutor.
- Around Town: Take a class in CPR at a local YMCA or other recreation center.

ing new technology so that they can focus on doing the jobs they were hired to do.

Similarly, changes in laws and business environments are critical areas for training. A company can be at risk if employees do not know the implications of things like harassment and discrimination laws, handicapped accommodations, accepting gifts from vendors, disclosing proprietary information, copyright and trademark regulations, and safety regulations. For example, consider the recent acceleration in using the toxic metal cadmium in children's jewelry. Employees that manufacture or import children's jewelry may require training to understand safety and legal risks associated with cadmium and learn how to accurately test for it. This knowledge is valuable for preventing recalls and lawsuits, and for keeping customers safe.

Corporate trainers usually work in the human resources department. They are among the first in the company to test new systems

and software. They research innovations and new issues that crop up in their fields, then combine that information with company needs to create training programs. If a company merger takes place, corporate trainers often take the lead in mixing new company cultures and expectations so there is no open hostility between factions.

Corporate trainers reach all employees in some way. They must be effective communicators who are credible experts in their fields. When the company is successful, trainers can take pride in doing their share to help everyone do their best work.

Correctional Educator

According to a *Corrections Today* report titled "The Top Nine Reasons to Increase Correctional Education" (Stephen Steurer, et al: August 2010), an overwhelming majority of prison inmates name education as a personal reentry need (https://www.aca.org/fileupload/177/ahaidar/Steurer.pdf). In other words, inmates want to learn. Many people lend their teaching services to those serving prison terms. Correctional institutions have a stake in providing inmate education, and many facilities see it as the right thing to do. Education can be used as a benefit that helps correctional officers run the jail, prison, or juvenile justice facility smoothly. Additionally, prisoners who keep learning have a better chance at successfully reentering society.

Student inmates' educational levels run the full gamut from illiteracy to those who aspire to college or graduate degrees. Some students attend classes voluntarily, while others are required to be there (especially juvenile students, who are subject to the same educational privileges and requirements as they would have been had they remained in school). Students range from minimum-security offenders to death row prisoners. The variety makes it challenging for correctional educators to set curriculum and expectations.

GET STARTED NOW!

- In School: College prep, plus public speaking and communications.
- After School: Volunteer to tutor peers in your favorite subject. Ask to sit in on an adult literacy class at a vocational school or other learning center.
- Around Town: Interview a correctional educator to find out what his day-to-day job is like.

CAREER 411

Search It!
Correctional Education Association at http://www.ceanational.org/index2.htm.

Surf It!
Find out about art teachers in prison at http://www.huffingtonpost.com/daniel-grant/artists-as-teachers-in-pr_b_565695.html.

Read It!
Read a blog about teaching writing inside of a prison: http://teachingontheinside.wordpress.com.

Learn It!
Minimum Education: Bachelor's degree, some jobs require teaching certificate and master's degree.

Typical Majors: Teaching, English, math, languages, history, science, art, vocational education.

Special Skills: Patience, flexibility, desire to help others, ability to interact with people from many cultures and backgrounds, organizational skills, excellent communication skills.

Earn It!
Median annual salary is $51,370.
(Source: http://www.salaryexpert.com)

Possible classes for inmates can include general literacy, GED (general equivalency diplomas), and vocational or technical education. Prisons can provide life skills classes such as anger management, personal finance, parenting skills, and job-search skills. Prisons may also offer enrichment classes in art, music, dance, or theater.

In some cases correctional facilities accept volunteer teachers with limited experience; other facilities require advanced teaching degrees and extensive experience, particularly when teaching government-sponsored and GED classes. Correctional facilities sometimes partner with local universities and community colleges or with nonprofit organizations like museums, to provide more teachers and a diverse, high-quality course selection.

So, what is a day in the life of a correctional educator like? You may be checked into the prison like any other visitor. At first you will probably receive training about what to expect, and how to behave with the prison population. Then you will teach your classes. As a reading and English instructor, for example, you may first teach basic reading, then work on literature essays with GED students, then oversee a group reading of a play. Like other teachers you will assess each student's needs and evaluate their progress.

Working with the prison population requires patience and flexibility. You will encounter students from many different cultures and ethnic groups. You will probably encounter some violent offenders, too. Some will have limited language and social abilities, while others may have special needs. Like any other class-

IF YOU WERE. . .

As a correctional educator, how would you teach job interview skills to a prison population?

. . . MAKE IT REAL!

Read about how to prepare for a job interview at http://www.howstuffworks.com/search.php?terms=job+interview. Then create a lesson plan around it for adult prisoners. Keep the unusual needs of your audience in mind as you think of interesting ways to convey the information and provide role-playing experiences for them.

room, some students will be happy to be there and others will not. But also like in any other classroom, knowing you have helped one of these students get a degree, learn to read, or just feel more confident gives great personal satisfaction.

Distance Learning Coordinator

Have you ever taken a course online? If you haven't, you are not alone—yet. Distance learning-related jobs are projected to grow much faster than normal. With technological advancements helping us connect more easily, teachers and students are taking advantage of being able to "go" to class in their pajamas. It is the job of the distance learning coordinator to make this possible.

Distance learning coordinators first assess needs and goals of the institutions or corporations they work for. For example, if you work for a university, you may analyze data to find out which academic areas will draw in a lot of students online, and focus your energy on those. If you already have instructors in place, your next step might be to make a class schedule and obtain course descriptions, using instructional design principles to make classes efficient and appealing at the same time.

Once you finalize course offerings, you need to schedule when and how students and teachers will meet for each class. It helps to use online course management software, video conferencing and Web casting, virtual libraries, and other means for students and

GET STARTED NOW!

- In School: Computer classes, graphic design, business classes. If possible, take an online course to see what the experience is like.
- After School: Try your hand at designing a Web site or starting a blog.
- Around Town: Volunteer for a nonprofit or charity that has on online component, such as a newsletter, interactive blog, or social media page.

teachers to network and communicate informally. For some parts of the classes, students may need to physically visit some classrooms and labs, lectures, study groups or other hands-on experiences. Finally, you will need to help instructors translate their course materials into Web-accessible documents.

When you figure out how students and the teacher will attend class together virtually, you can open up registration. Once students have signed up, you can train their teachers and them to use all the cool stuff—libraries, videos, chat rooms, etc. You provide tech support by troubleshooting any problems that arise as students "go" to class, or alert them to any changes with facilities or scheduling.

As a distance learning coordinator, you may have to maintain the distance-learning program as a whole, and analyze how successful each class was. You may build databases of participating students and teachers, assess their success and satisfaction, and even create virtual tours, Web sites, and other marketing materials to promote distance learning.

Distance learning is a new, growing job sector. It is a "green" career, since students and teachers don't need to travel to classes, and it cuts down on paper use. And, since students and teachers are already communicating electronically, it encourages more informal interaction and on-the-spot tutoring for students who need it. Since entire virtual schools and universities are springing up, learning to be a distance learning coordinator offers great odds for getting a job.

Driving Instructor

Do you remember how nervous you were when you first got behind the wheel of a car? What was your driving instructor like? Most likely, the instructor was relaxed. They have to be; they get into cars with new drivers every day, and screaming just does not help anyone. Driving instructors give students one of the most important gifts they will ever have—FREEDOM!—and knowledge about how to be safe on the road.

There are a few different types of driving instructors. High school driving instructors can teach in high schools, they can oversee online courses, or they can work for private driving schools. Some of these instructors can only teach the in-car driving portion of the class. Others can teach both the in-car portion and the in-class portion. Other, specialized driving instructors teach people to drive motorcycles or 18-wheeler trucks. Some lucky instructors even teach racecar driving to people who want to try out a track for fun, or who want to learn to compete in racing.

A day in the life of a typical high school driving instructor may start with teaching in the classroom. Your job is to make sure students understand state driver's license requirements and national driving regulations. You will teach them to identify traffic signs and what to do in a variety of driving situations. In the afternoon, or even at night, you take students out in a driving instructor car. The car usually has a sign on it that indicates a student driver is

GET STARTED NOW!

- In School: Participate in any driver's education programs your school offers.
- After School: Get involved in (or establish) a local chapter of Students Against Drunk Driving (http://www.sadd.org).
- Around Town: Practice safe driving habits!

CAREER 411

Search It!
Visit the American Driver and Traffic Safety Education Association at http://www.adtsea.org/adtsea.

Surf It!
Try some tricky driving at Driver's Ed Direct at http://www.driverseddirect.com/drivinggame/driving-game.asp.

Read It!
Find out more about safe driving with the article "Top 10 Safe Driving Tips" at http://auto.howstuffworks.com/car-driving-safety/accidents-hazardous-conditions/10-safe-driving-tips.htm.

Learn It!
Minimum Education: High school diploma for in-car instructors, bachelor's degree or specialized degree for in-class instructors, plus a good driving record.

Typical Majors: Education, post-secondary education, or specialized driver's education.

Special Skills: Patience, calm disposition, attention to detail, excellent communication skills, active listening skills, and excellent driving skills.

Earn It!
Median annual salary is $32,553.

(Source: http://www.payscale.com)

behind the wheel. (Get off the sidewalk!) The car may be equipped with a special brake on the passenger's side, in case the student hits the gas instead of the brake. You may take students through a special training course, and then out on the open road. While driving test requirements differ from state to state, most students need to know how to park, do a three-point turn, back up safely, merge and accelerate, obey all traffic signs, and come to a complete stop. Some even tackle parallel parking,

Driving instructor training and requirements vary from state to state. Most states require teachers to be at least 21 and have a clean driving record, so it is a good idea to obey traffic rules and avoid speeding tickets and accidents if you aspire to be a driving instructor—or even if you don't. Driving instructors must have high school diplomas (for in-car instruction) and bachelor's degrees or teacher training (for in-car and in-class instruction). It also helps to have nerves of steel. Even though students will be much more nervous than you are, covering your eyes in fear while they creep (or screech) down the road will not help them at all.

Elementary School Teacher

Today is field trip day. First you call a couple of parents whose kids did not bring permission forms. Next you greet students and the parents who volunteered to chaperone, then board the bus and head to the county fair. You walk students through the agriculture building to snag some popcorn, pick up helmets at the firefighter's station, and then sit down to watch a sheepdog demonstration. After lunch at the fair, you head back to school in time for music class and a little journal writing. After dismissal, you check parent conference times, prepare tomorrow's math lesson, and schedule a yearbook meeting with the principal, since you are heading that committee this year.

An elementary school's teacher's job is to give students a firm foundation in reading and language arts, writing, math, science, social studies, and sometimes art, music, and physical education. Today many classrooms are interactive, with discussions, group

GET STARTED NOW!

- In School: Take psychology, child development, and communications classes. Also consider physical education, art, and music, since many students learn academic content through these experiences.
- After School: Join the Future Educators Association, organized by Phi Delta Kappa International, to help students explore careers in education: http://www.futureeducators.org/index.htm.
- Around Town: Volunteer at a local elementary school, after-school care program, or youth sports organization to get used to working with children.

CAREER 411

Search It!
The National Association for Educators of Young Children at http://www.naeyc.org.

Surf It!
Get acquainted with nationally recognized teachers at http://programs.ccsso.org/projects/national_teacher_of_the_year/national_teachers.

Read It!
Learn more about becoming a teacher in your state at http://certificationmap.com.

Learn It!
Minimum Education: Bachelor's degree plus state certification.

Typical Majors: Elementary education, child development, child psychology.

Special Skills: Interest in children, patience, flexibility, excellent communication skills, excellent organizational skills, critical thinking.

Earn It!
Median annual salary is $50,510.
(Source: U.S. Department of Labor)

work, and hands-on learning. Although states mandate curriculum standards, good teachers plan creative activities that make it fun to learn. Every student learns differently, so teachers must adjust teaching and discipline methods accordingly. A teacher is held accountable, along with students and parents, for how well students perform on tests, how much they learn, and how well they behave in class.

Elementary school teachers may teach in private or public schools. Private schools must receive accreditation from an approved state or regional association. District (public) schools are largely funded by taxpayers. Students are assigned to schools based on their addresses, or through lotteries or other school choice programs. Within public schools are charter and magnet schools. Charter schools are tailored to community needs and are partially funded by organizations and individuals. Magnet schools focus on a particular discipline or philosophy, like science or multiple intelligences.

Teachers are also responsible for identifying students who have special needs due to physical, emotional, or learning disabilities, and referring them for services to improve their school experiences. Teachers meet with parents, supervisors and colleagues

IF YOU WERE. . .

As an elementary school teacher preparing a science unit on clouds, how could you make the learning experience especially enjoyable and effective for your students?

. . . MAKE IT REAL!

Rev up your imagination and use resources such as Education World (http://www.educationworld.com) to gather information about your topic. Then make a plan for how to introduce the content to students, prepare activities students can engage in to master the content, and find a creative way to evaluate what students have learned.

about
matters per-
taining to teach-
ing and to running
the school. Day-to-day activities
include grading papers, preparing for standardized testing, and
assigning grades. Teachers may also
be responsible for extracurricular assignments, such as directing
programs, hosting science night or curriculum night, and tutoring. After school, teachers must complete report card comments,
work on lesson plans, and stay current on teaching methods and
standards.

Being an elementary school teacher is about supporting students' development—academic, social, and emotional. Elementary
school teachers play a huge role in children's lives; your parents
and grandparents probably still remember their early teachers'
names better than the names of their college professors. Bear this
in mind as you choose this profession. Your students will always
remember you, so be sure to make a great impression.

English as a Second Language (ESL) Teacher

English is an easy language to speak, read, and understand—if you grew up with it. It is difficult to learn English language and culture if you grew up in another part of the world. For one thing, English has many exceptions to standardized rules. Take a verb like "to be." Instead of saying "I be, you be, he be," we say "I am, you are, he is." Think about how nonnative speakers might interpret an idiom like "She drives me up the wall." ESL teachers help with both linguistic and cultural transitions.

Speaking English well does not qualify you to teach it. Teaching nonnative speakers to speak, read, and write in English requires training and certification. Many ESL teachers teach a combination of language basics (grammar, vocabulary, spelling, and pronunciation) and cultural awareness. It helps to know how to explain your native language and culture by making comparisons students can understand. Combining language proficiency with an understanding of cultural norms helps to give nonnative speakers confidence.

For example, you may have ESL college students from many countries, like Japan, Morocco, Thailand, Germany, and Rus-

GET STARTED NOW!

- In School: Take foreign language courses, world geography courses, and psychology.
- After School: Join a foreign language club, and travel abroad if you can to experience what it is like to be a nonnative speaker.
- Around Town: Sit in on or volunteer with a class where ESL is taught to adults or children. Community organizations and community colleges may offer these experiences.

sia. As you teach a basic handshake and greeting like "Hello. How are you," you explain the words and gestures. In the United States it is customary to accompany a firm but brief handshake with eye contact. Firm handshakes and eye contact are customary for Russians and Germans. The Japanese student will probably know foreigners expect to shake hands, but may still bow as well. A student from Thailand may make the *wai*, a gesture of greeting made with palms touching as if in prayer. The Moroccan student may prefer a gentler handshake. Contrasting these norms with American greetings helps students know what to say and how to say it.

ESL teachers have a world of opportunities open to them. They can teach in elementary and secondary schools, in universities, or in adult education programs. Students may be of any age; some ESL teachers in the United States work with school children, while others teach recently immigrated adults, or teach executives whose companies have sent them abroad to learn English. They can even teach English in other countries. ESL teachers may teach classes specialized for a specific purpose, such as to help foreign-born doctors converse with patients, or teach children how to communicate with classmates.

Teaching English to nonnative speakers can be very rewarding. Students can become frustrated and homesick, but learning the language can help them through this. Although teaching abroad is a great way to learn about other cultures, such teachers may receive low salaries. Many English language learners prefer to learn British English, so teachers must adjust accordingly, but being able to have good conversations with students is very rewarding. You will be as proud of them as they are of themselves.

Environmental Educator

Work outdoors! Save the earth! Teach people to care about the environment! As an environmental educator, you can do these things while enjoying the great outdoors. On any given day, you may be hiking, diving, climbing, or canoeing with students. Environmental education is a huge and varied field, so here are a few of the many options.

As an environmental center educator, one of the many occupations in this field, you would create, coordinate, and teach programs to students and teachers. You may work in labs or at outside locations like streams, oceans, deserts, or wetlands. You may host visiting student groups, and design programs for summer campers as well. Environmental center educators need a bachelor's degree in environmental science, usually combined with an education degree.

Park rangers protect life, conserve resources, and educate visitors in national parks. Some duties include fee collection and law enforcement, but many rangers teach natural, historic, or scientific information tailored to each park. For example, at Yellowstone Park you could lead 4th–8th graders on a five-day hiking trip to

GET STARTED NOW!

- In School: Take science courses, especially biology, physical science, earth science, environmental science, world geography, and marine science.
- After School: Since you may be responsible for students on outdoor trips, take CPR and basic first-aid training.
- Around Town: Volunteer or get a summer job at a local park or nature center. Take up hiking, canoeing, kayaking, climbing, or another outdoor sport.

CAREER 411

Search It!
North American Association for Environmental Educators at http://www.naaee.org.

Surf It!
Take a crash course in environmental science at http://science.howstuffworks.com/environmental.

Read It!
Learn more about national parks from this Discovery Channel article at http://dsc.discovery.com/guides/national-parks/national-park.html.

Learn It!
Minimum Education: Bachelor's degree, master's degree for some positions.

Typical Majors: Biology, marine biology, environmental science, earth science, physical science, zoology, natural resources conservation, forestry.

Special Skills: Strong communication skills, active lifestyle, ability to work alone or as part of a team, observational skills, problem-solving abilities, leadership skills.

Earn It!
Median annual salary is $60,160.
(Source: U.S. Department of Labor)

do field investigations. In the Florida Everglades you could take visitors on a "slough slog" through the grass and river to discover local species. It is the ranger's job to protect the park's plant and animal life, and to keep visitors safe and informed. A two-year associate's degree is the minimum requirement for this position. (Since you are out in the wilderness, cardiopulmonary resuscitation (CPR) training and emergency medical technician (EMT) certification are helpful.)

A marine biologist educator coordinates coastal and marine educational efforts, often in conjunction with federally funded programs. Marine biologist educators organize beach and underwater cleanups, monitor marine animal and plant species, lead diving or canoe expeditions, and teach groups how to help conserve the marine environment. A marine biologist might, for example, run a sea turtle hospital, demonstrate how baby turtles are cared for, and take groups to see nest sites while teaching visitors how not to disturb them. Marine biologists have undergraduate and graduate science degrees, and often hold education degrees, too.

Other environmental educators work with corporations, or with the public, to promote understanding of consumers' and industries' impact on the environment. For example, they may

IF YOU WERE. . .

As an environmental educator for a local science center, what would you teach your summer visitors about local wildlife?

. . . MAKE IT REAL!

Research local wildlife, and choose one species that interests you. Prepare an animal lesson plan for elementary students. Include a photo or illustration, the animal's typical size, diet, and nesting habits. Make sure to include a few fun facts and a kid-friendly activity in your lesson plan.

help dishwasher manufacturers understand the importance of water conservation, or create public service announcements about ways to conserve water in the home. They may create environmental consciousness programs to raise corporate and public awareness of national and global environmental issues. These educators have at least a bachelor's degree in science, and often have teacher training as well.

As our growing population puts strain on our natural resources, we need environmental educators to teach us how to conserve those resources and protect the world's dwindling natural areas. Applying teaching skills to this purpose also means that you get paid to play outside!

Guidance Counselor

CAREER 411

Search It!
American School Counselor Association at http://www. schoolcounselor.org.

Surf It!
Look at some positive problem-solving models for kids, like this fun children's quiz on PBS Kids at http://pbskids.org/arthur/ games/yougottobekidding.

Read It!
Find more information about becoming a guidance counselor on the U.S. College Search Web site at http://www. uscollegesearch.org/blog/category/ becoming-a-guidance-counselor.

Learn It!
Minimum Education: Master's degree.

Typical Majors: Psychology or child psychology, social work, behavioral sciences.

Special Skills: Desire to help people, active listening skills, tolerance for stress, dependability, integrity, discretion, excellent organizational skills.

Earn It!
Median annual salary is $52,550.

(Source: U.S. Department of Labor)

You have an open-door policy as a guidance counselor. You talk with all kinds of students: those who are having arguments with their friends, those whose home life makes it tough to do well in school, those who do not know whether they want to go to college, and even those who just want advice about career paths. All students are important to you, and their problems matter, regardless of how large or how small.

If you are in high school, you may only go to your school guidance counselor for class schedule changes or to get a college application, but a guidance counselor's job extends beyond that. At all grade levels school counselors create an atmosphere of safety and trust throughout the school, and especially in their offices. They help with career planning and college applications, and work with students to manage social, behavioral, and personal issues.

Elementary school guidance counselors often meet with classes to discuss things like friendship and good behavior strategies. Counselors also help teachers evaluate individual children for disabilities or other issues that require intervention and special services. When guidance counselors become aware of cur-

GET STARTED NOW!

- In School: Psychology, social studies, communications, and public speaking.
- After School: Meet with your school guidance counselor to find out how she chose this field, what the challenges and rewards of the job are, and what she recommends for someone who wants to pursue guidance counseling as a career.
- Around Town: Volunteer to tutor younger students, or to babysit, so you get some hands-on experience working with youth.

rent or potential problems, they work with parents, teachers, and administrators to develop helpful strategies for the classroom and home. If an issue is serious enough or stems from problems in the home, the guidance counselor may refer the case to a school social worker, school psychologist, or an outside agency.

Middle school students are often affected by physical, social, and psychological transitions that happen during the early teen years. Counselors provide a safe and trusting atmosphere in which students can seek help and support. They also lead parents, teachers, and administrators to support students who need special services.

High school guidance counselors address a diverse set of challenges. In some schools, separate counselors help with career exploration and college applications, and advise students

about course requirements for future jobs. Counselors may also work to ensure students' overall mental health by advising students who are involved in disciplinary cases, helping with substance abuse problems, coordinating teen pregnancy support and prevention programs, and working to reduce dropout rates. Guidance counselors are often called upon to make and adjust class schedules, disseminate information about careers, colleges, and admissions tests, coordinate college and career fairs, help students with financial aid applications, and discuss the implications of admissions tests scores.

Guidance counselors fulfill a very important role for students. They help with practical tasks, and also help students navigate their way through difficult parts of life at school. Many students find it reassuring knowing that help is just behind the guidance counselor's door. As a guidance counselor, you won't be able to solve all of the problems immediately, but you will be able to inspire parents, teachers, and students to tackle them with the right resources and knowledge.

Instructional Coordinator

It's summer. School is out. Students and teachers alike are enjoying a much needed break. But there you are, making sure that everything is ready when everyone comes back. Last week you ordered new lab computers, scheduled training sessions about the new fourth-grade math test requirements, and evaluated two new textbooks. Today you have a meeting with your principal to select and purchase new fifth-grade social studies atlases that reflect recent population and demographic shifts. Tomorrow you meet with three new kindergarten teachers to review the lesson plans they have prepared. You have suggestions from all of them. With these adjustments your school will still be top notch.

Teachers cannot possibly keep up with everything happening outside of the classroom that affects how and what they teach, and still do their teaching jobs. National and state governments periodically create new curriculum guidelines. Standardized test content changes. Researchers find more effective ways to help students understand certain concepts. To that, add changes in the job market that make certain skills more or less important, and changes in technology that leave seasoned teachers playing catch-up with their students. How is a teacher to keep up?

GET STARTED NOW!

- In School: College prep, public speaking, communications.
- After School: Go online to the Web sites of the publishers of some of your school textbooks. Notice the key selling points for each textbook. Do you think your district's instructional coordinator made a good choice?
- Around Town: Visit a local school-supply store. Look at the amazing variety of resources available to help educate students.

CAREER 411

Search It!
The Association for Supervision and Curriculum Development at http://www.ascd.org.

Surf It!
Experiment with a lesson-plan building tool at http://www.teach-nology.com/web_tools/lesson_plan.

Read It!
Explore what works in education at the George Lucas Educational Foundation at http://www.edutopia.org.

Learn It!
Minimum Education: Master's degree.

Typical Majors: Education, curriculum and instruction, educational technology, or a content area such as reading or math.

Special Skills: Excellent research skills, teaching experience, communication skills, decision-making skills, ability to use technology, leadership, and initiative.

Earn It!
Median annual salary is $58,780.
(Source: U.S. Department of Labor)

Fortunately instructional coordinators, also called curriculum specialists, stay informed of all of these changes by reviewing the educational programs in each district, school, or department. They make sure that classroom instruction meets the required goals or standards, as well as students' needs. Instructional coordinators may specialize in different areas, like elementary, middle, or high school; gifted education; special education; technology; or vocational training.

When they are not working in classrooms, instructional coordinators have plenty to do outside of the classroom. They evaluate teaching materials that schools plan to buy, like lab equipment, computer software, and textbooks. Why? Well, lab equipment wears out. Software changes constantly. Science discoveries keep happening. Innovations like the Internet create a greater need for newer computers. Textbooks change due to shifts in population and social attitudes. Instructional coordinators keep these changes in mind as they review available options, confer with teacher reviewers, and recommend investing large sums of money in new school supplies. They also conduct teacher-training ses-

IF YOU WERE. . .

As an instructional coordinator, how would you design a five-day unit to teach third-grade students about the solar system using only free online resources?

. . . MAKE IT REAL!

Search some teacher-friendly Web sites, like PBS (http://www.pbs.org) and How Stuff Works (http://www.howstuffworks.com), and teacher lesson-plan sites like Lesson Planz (http://www.lessonplanz.com). Create a five-lesson curriculum guide with a one-page summary of each lesson plan, including the materials and resources you will use.

sions so they can share the best new teaching practices and techniques they learn in the course of their research.

Clearly the job of the instructional coordinator matters. Every
purchase and teacher-training session will touch the lives of many
teachers and their students. The materials coordinators select or
create and the teachers that they train will serve (or fail to serve)
students in a school or district for years to come.

Instructional Media Designer

Your mom gave you her old car. She expects you to take care of it. Now the oil light is on. You want to change it yourself, so you look up your favorite brand of oil and watch an online video that shows how to safely raise the car, drain the old oil, properly dispose of it, and add new oil. With help from a friend and some tools, you get the job done right. Congratulations! You have just successfully used instructional media. And hey, you saved $25!

An entire industry is springing up around instructional media, ranging from informal how-to videos to learning games and online school presentations. Instructional media designers create media that teach people how to do almost anything, like changing oil or working on math problems.

Many adults now choose to pursue degrees online. Some instructional media designers create online components for classes. Designing educational media can be as simple as making videos of teachers teaching then posting the videos on a university Web site. In other cases instructional media designers must research potential courses and create multimedia presentations and even game-based learning that complements core instruc-

GET STARTED NOW!

- In School: Computer design, graphic design, film production classes, communications, media arts.
- After School: Volunteer to direct a school play or record video at the school talent show.
- Around Town: Visit the Web site of a local college, university, or local high school. Check to see if there is a virtual tour that both shows and tells you about the school.

tion. For example, a college-level math course might include an online math game for students to use to practice core concepts. Due to the variety of needs, instructional media designers should be proficient in audio and video recording, as well as graphic design, media production, and in computer languages (Javascript, Dreamweaver, etc.).

Another type of instructional media is the "how-to" video. If a hardware store hires you to create a how-to video for installing floor tile, you oversee the production and use live action or animation to show step-by-step instructions for choosing tile, preparing the surface, laying and cutting tile, grouting, and clean-up—using (and advertising) the store's products. Customers can click on the live video to learn which products to use and how to use them.

Finally, many corporations train employees with instructional media. For example, a hospital might require new EMT personnel to watch a virtual tour of the hospital's Emergency Room check-in procedures and traffic flow. Or a car manufacturer may need a video presentation to train factory employees about new seat-belt installation techniques. Instructional media designers make sure that everyone gets consistent information.

At the minimum, instructional media designers meet with teachers or companies to find out how long instruction should be, what information to include, and whether live action, animation, or something like PowerPoint is most appropriate. Many go the extra mile by interviewing experts to gather information, or by helping instructors integrate media with their face-to-face training, to ensure that the media are compatible with the rest of the instruction being offered. For those who love to combine learning and technology, this career promises an excellent growth outlook and a tremendous amount of variety.

Museum Education Coordinator

Your career as a museum education coordinator has been very... well, educational. You have interned for the Toy Museum of New York and the Smithsonian National Museum of Natural History (in the dinosaur department). You have worked for the Modern Art Museum of Fort Worth, the Baseball Hall of Fame, and the San Diego Air and Space Museum. Now you work in Colonial Williamsburg, a Virginian village preserved since the Revolutionary War. Today you will lead a third-grade class in churning butter, and then take them on a tour of the museum's vegetable gardens. Your job is to make sure that visitors learn a lot and enjoy themselves, too.

Museum education coordinators help people understand and learn from museum collections and programs. Their most visible programs are guided tours. No tour can cover every item, so the coordinator selects a representative sample of items, plans an interesting and logical order for the tour, and creates guided tours or lesson plans that explain each item and its relationship

GET STARTED NOW!

- In School: Use electives to explore interest areas that might lead to a job in a museum. Consider art appreciation, music, history, or science.
- After School: Volunteer at a local museum and find out how they procure, display, and store materials.
- Around Town: Tour several different kinds of museums to find out what tour guides emphasize on the tours, and to understand the different kinds of museums available.

CAREER 411

Search It!
American Association of Museums at http://www.aam-us.org and Museum-Ed at http://www.museum-ed.org.

Surf It!
Try these fun games sponsored by the Tate Gallery Museum in London, England, at http://kids.tate.org.uk/games/.

Read It!
Find information about museum studies training programs at http://museumstudies.si.edu/courses.html.

Learn It!
Minimum Education: Bachelor's degree.

Typical Majors: Education or a subject area related to museums, such as art history, humanities, history, or science.

Special Skills: Excellent research and organizational skills, strong communication skills, flexibility, adaptability, ability to work well with others, creativity.

Earn It!
Median annual salary is $36,270.
(Source: U.S. Department of Labor)

to the collection. The education coordinator may create different tours and lessons for different grade levels, for the general public, and for certain audiences, like scientists, historians, or artists, that have more background in the collection's subject area. The education coordinator creates and scripts tours, and then trains staff and volunteers to present them.

Creating tours is just one part of a museum education coordinator's task. The coordinator also provides background materials for classroom teachers to use before the museum visit. For the public,

the coordinator may create brochures or materials for self-guided tours. Most of this information will also be added to the museum Web site. Additionally museum education coordinators may set up workshops, lectures, or film series that relate to an exhibition or to the museum's general mission, and may coordinate classes for the museum to offer, such as studio art and art appreciation.

Some museum education coordinators specialize in writing and editing print articles for a museum magazine, or online materials, such as a blog, for museum members. Articles may reference current exhibits or contain more general information about the museum. Coordinators can also create labels, brochures, and catalogs, as well as annual reports, newsletters, and public relations press releases designed to further educate the public about the museum.

As public and private organizations emphasize establishing archives and organizing records and information, and as public interest in science, art, history, and technology increases, museum education coordinators can expect opportunities to increase, especially, perhaps, in smaller, more specialized museums. If there is an area of art, nature, science, or history that you love, work to become an expert in it, and consider becoming a museum educational coordinator as a way to share that special knowledge.

Physical Fitness Trainer

CAREER 411

Search It!
IDEA Health and Fitness Association at http://www.ideafit.com or the National Aerobics and Fitness Trainers Association at http://www.nafta1.com.

Surf It!
Practice living healthy by printing out and filling in this food and fitness diary at http://www.womenshealth.gov/bodyworks/toolkit/toolkit.teens.pdf.

Read It!
Use this list of resources from the President's Council on Physical Fitness and Sports to find articles about health and fitness at http://www.fitness.gov/resources_health.htm.

Learn It!
Minimum Education: Specialized training with certification.

Typical Majors: Exercise science, physical education, kinesiology (study of body movement), education.

Special Skills: Love of physical activity, desire to help people, leadership, teaching, time management, analytical, problem-solving skills.

Earn It!
Median annual salary is $30,670.

(Source: U.S. Department of Labor)

Physical fitness is a relatively new concept. Commuting, desk jobs, and sedentary activities like surfing the Net have conspired to help people become less active, and therefore, less healthy. Also, physicians have discovered that physical activity can prevent or slow some diseases, and speed recovery, as well. Increasing awareness of the pitfalls of a sedentary lifestyle is drawing increasing numbers of people into gyms and fitness centers, thus creating a growing need for fitness professionals who assist clients in setting and reaching fitness goals.

Physical fitness trainers work in many different environments. For example, as an exercise physiologist—a specialized fitness trainer—at a university, your daily responsibilities might include building fitness conditioning for athletes. At a hospital you could devise therapy exercise programs to help patients recover from treatment or fight chronic diseases. Clinically oriented fitness centers help clients who are more at risk (such as patients on chemotherapy) safely return to an active and fit lifestyle. In these and other scenarios, trainers can provide nutritional education to address clients' total health outlook.

GET STARTED NOW!

- In School: Take anatomy and physiology, health and nutrition, biology, and physical fitness classes.
- After School: Play some sports, since fitness trainers are often responsible for enforcing rules and regulations for organized sports at recreation and fitness centers.
- Around Town: Visit a few fitness centers in town and ask for a tour. If possible, interview a trainer about his or her education and experience.

Some trainers prefer to work for a personal training or fitness studio, so they can run their businesses without a ton of administrative headaches. As a trainer in a fitness studio, you might bark orders at a group of clients who want to lose weight in a boot-camp atmosphere. You would assess their needs and then design aerobic activities that suit their abilities, such as swimming and movement classes, and strength training exercises to enable weight loss. You would demonstrate the exercise equipment and the proper way to breathe as you cheer on your clients and track their progress. You would also provide nutrition information to speed the process, all the while making sure students pursue their goals in a safe and healthy manner.

Some trainers teach CPR and basic lifesaving training classes, or provide clients with nutrition and other wellness information. A trainer might be asked to help with "fun runs" or other community events, either to publicize the facility or to benefit a charity. And a trainer would file injury and accident reports, and oversee health screenings like flu shot sessions or mammography screenings (if working with a medical facility). The physical fitness coordinator must also maintain the facility's budget and keep records of expenditures and of class and facility attendance, to help the facility determine whether it is meeting budget requirements and clients' needs.

Pursing a career in physical fitness gives you a rare career opportunity to get paid for staying in shape. With widespread concern about growing rates of obesity among children and adults, and increasing emphasis on the health benefits associated with fitness, there is plenty of opportunity on the horizon for fitness trainers.

Preschool Teacher

Walk into a preschool classroom and you'll see little kids having what looks like one giant play date. A few kids are on the carpet driving trucks and building roads with blocks. Three children are giggling as their teacher dips their feet in paint and makes footprints on paper. Two other children wrestle over one doll while a teacher asks them to share. Two children are scooping up dried rice in measuring cups at the water table. What you are really seeing are future architects, mechanics, civil engineers, artists, parents, childcare workers, scientists, and chefs. All that "play" is actually very hard work. A good preschool experience lays the foundation for future success.

Preschool teachers plan each day's activities. They often base activities around a theme, which can be simple, like apples, or complex, like castles. Teachers take great care to include art, music, language and literacy, math, science and social studies, and gross- and fine-motor activities in order to give students a well-rounded experience. Students also learn self-help skills: zipping jackets, opening lunch containers, and using the restroom independently. The preschool teacher may work with individual students, small groups, or the whole class.

Socialization is a crucial area of preschool development. Preschoolers' growing ability to relate to each other prepares them

GET STARTED NOW!

- In School: Child development, psychology, English (children's literature).
- After School: Look for a part-time job in a child-care center or after-school care program.
- Around Town: Volunteer to work with children. Babysit, become a preschool camp counselor, or work in the nursery at your place of worship.

CAREER 411

Search It!
National Association for the Education of Young Children at http://www.naeyc.org.

Surf It!
Visit the Nick Jr. television channel Web site and play some preschool-directed games at http://www.nickjr.com/games/index.jhtml.

Read It!
TeachersFirst has a wonderful list of children's books at http://www.teachersfirst.com/100books.cfm. Choose a few interesting books to read or reread some of your own childhood favorites.

Learn It!
Minimum Education: Associate's degree.

Typical Majors: Early childhood education, child development, child psychology.

Special Skills: Patience, energy, ability to multitask, excellent organizational skills, desire to help others, stress tolerance, excellent listening and communication skills.

Earn It!
Median annual salary is $24,540.

(Source: U.S. Department of Labor)

for other kinds of learning. Young toddlers start with parallel play (playing near other kids, and occasionally sharing toys—or fighting over them) to fully engaged one-on-one and group play. Preschool teachers frequently resolve conflicts between children, and help them build trusting friendships with each other and with their teachers.

In addition to center-based preschool programs, people also provide child care in their homes. Home-based childcare providers care for small groups of children while parents are at work. Most states require fairly strict registration and certification processes for legally providing at-home child care.

Currently, many children have no access to quality preschool education, and preschool teachers earn significantly less than kindergarten teachers. However, educational groups are encouraging policy makers to implement high standards for preschools by increasing pay and benefits, thereby making the profession more competitive. Despite potentially low pay, being a preschool teacher is a rigorous profession. You must be able to quickly get to children who need you, and bring calm to the chaos that comes with managing a lot of kids. You also have to care for children with spe-

IF YOU WERE. . .

As a preschool teacher working with two-year-olds, how would you deal with the common behavioral issue of biting?

. . . MAKE IT REAL!

Use the Internet to research the topic of preschool biting. Use the information you discover to create an official biting policy for your class. Include strategies for dealing with both the biters and bitten (including first-aid practices). Be specific with scripts and consistent responses for dealing with this problem.

cial needs, such as disabilities, separation anxiety, and even severe allergies to foods such as milk and peanuts. It takes a special person to deal patiently and kindly with students who need so much care. On some days it will seem like every child in your classroom is crying, fighting, getting sick, or whining for Mama. But on the good days, getting a smile from a child or seeing a student learn to share nicely with friends is a huge payoff.

Principal

For school principals, the day starts long before the first bell rings. Today is no exception. You start early by completing a few teacher evaluations. After you help another student deliver the morning announcements, you interview a potential new hire who may take over for your geometry teacher, who is moving. Next you have a lunch meeting with the superintendent to discuss funding for an addition to your building. (Good thing it's raining—the superintendent will have to splash out to the pod classrooms!) Next you will squeeze in more teacher evaluations, and then you have an appointment with the guidance counselor to talk about his progress with students' college application meetings. With such a full day, if any students misbehave, they will have to visit the assistant principal instead of you!

The essence of the principal's job is to create a school environment where students and teachers are safe, secure, and educated to their full potential. Principals must be big-picture people who can guide the school according to a particular vision and mission, but who can also address individual problems with care and concern. Principals must know about educational strategies, financial and legal issues, administration and organiza-

GET STARTED NOW!

- In School: College prep, debate, psychology, sociology.
- After School: Get involved in student government, or volunteer to help a teacher and find out a little more about how your school operates behind the scenes.
- Around Town: Attend a school board meeting to find out what issues might affect your school and your principal.

tional management, public relations, and group and individual psychology.

A principal is accountable for ensuring a high level of education. The principal interviews and hires teachers and staff, observes and evaluates teachers in action, and provides teachers with professional development so that they can keep learning. The principal also sets other educational standards, such as how students are grouped into classes, and grading guidelines. The principal reports test scores, explains budget use and shortfalls, and shares plans for improvement with the school board and the superintendent (if it is a public school).

Principals also implement policies and goals that affect the tone of the school. For example, they determine how much to emphasize physical education and athletics, or whether the school will position itself as a leader in technology, the arts, or another area. Principals also create school policies and ensure compliance with district policies on everything from Internet use, to emergency procedures in case of dangerous weather or a school intruder, to electives offered, to dress codes. A good principal also builds relationships outside of the school by encouraging programs that build parental involvement, creating good working relationships with local businesses and community groups, and making sure the school complies with legal regulations regarding special education, disaster planning, discipline, and continuing education.

If you walk through a school that is run by a good principal, you will see the evidence everywhere. Students are happy and well behaved, but not fearful. Teachers are energetic and motivated to work hard for their students. Parents are welcome and involved. The community knows what is going on at the school. An excellent school with these qualities is almost always led by an equally excellent principal.

Public Health Officer

If you had been born in 1900, you could expect to live to be 47. A baby born in the year 2000 can expect to live to age 77—that's 30 more years! Public health officers help prevent disease and promote health by providing information and encouraging behavioral changes. In other words, they tell us to get a flu shot, buckle up, put out that cigarette, and wash our hands at least 20 times a day. And we need to hear it! They must communicate clearly and persuasively, be good listeners and teachers, and overcome barriers of poverty, language, or cultural differences to help everyone take advantage of their services.

Public health officers can specialize in different areas. Environmental health workers keep our world clean. Biostatisticians analyze health-related data. Epidemiologists study the effects of contagious diseases like flu. Maternal and childcare experts help moms care for themselves and their babies. Nutrition experts teach the benefits of healthy eating. Health service administrators provide health screenings and advise insurance companies on policies. And behavioral scientists tell us how behaviors affect our health.

At corporations and worksites, public health officers may teach workplace safety—put on those hardhats! They share information

GET STARTED NOW!

- In School: Biology, chemistry, and behavioral sciences.
- After School: Volunteer in the school nurse's office to see what kinds of health issues crop up there.
- Around Town: Visit a public health clinic. If possible, make an appointment beforehand to interview an officer about his job.

CAREER 411

Search It!
The Association of Schools of Public Health at http://www.asph.org, the American Public Health Association at http://www.apha.org, or the Society for Public Health Education at http://www.sophe.org.

Surf It!
Get a quick overview of all of the things public health can do with this YouTube video called "This Is Public Health," at http://www.youtube.com/watch?v=Bpu42LmLo4U.

Read It!
Read a brochure from the Association of Schools of Public Health at http://www.asph.org/Publication/Reach/index.html. Or search for articles at the Centers for Disease Control and Prevention Web site at http://www.cdc.gov.

Learn It!
Minimum Education: Master's degree. Higher level jobs, like epidemiologists, require medical degrees.

Typical Majors: Nursing or public health.

Special Skills: Desire to help people, integrity, leadership, analytical thinking, problem-solving skills, dependability.

Earn It!
Median annual salary is $43,040.

(Source: U.S. Department of Labor)

about subjects like weight control or stress management, or inform workers about community health services like vaccination clinics.

City and state health department officers examine community health needs, evaluate existing health programs, and develop new ones. They organize and publicize screenings like blood pressure and cholesterol checks, and provide information about reducing disease outbreaks. They also promote safety information programs about things like using bicycle helmets or seat belts. It is common for schools, libraries, and volunteer organizations to ask public health officers to host classes for the community.

Within a community, officers work with individuals who share a common concern, like heart attack survivors or obese students. Officers could help heart patients change eating and exercise behavior, or work to add more fresh fruit and vegetable options to school cafeterias. To justify making changes, public health officers provide research that supports their ideas.

Many organizations obtain health officers' services. In private organizations like the American Cancer Society, public health educators develop campaigns and distribute materials addressing

IF YOU WERE. . .

As a public health officer, how would you educate parents about using child safety seats?

. . . MAKE IT REAL!

The laws for safety seats have recently changed. Research child safety seats on the Centers for Disease Control and Prevention Web site at http://www.cdc.gov/ ncipc/factsheets/childpas.htm. Then create an information poster, complete with artwork, about child restraint laws and how to properly use and install a car seat for an infant.

issues such as disease prevention and treatment options. Other groups like the World Health Organization employ officers to lead international health work and to educate people about such issues as epidemic prevention and control. Public health officers can also provide research data and participate on panels to help government agencies make informed decisions about health, wellness, and environmental issues.

Public health officers are important to populations who lack sufficient health care from other resources. They are also important to the general public as they keep an eye on potential epidemics and focus attention on wellness and disease prevention. Thanks to their efforts, many of us may be around a bit longer.

Public Librarian

As it says on the home page of the Public Library Association Web site, "Forget what you think you know about public librarians." Today's librarians' choices of places to work and responsibilities vary widely according to what customers want. Most of their responsibilities fall into three categories: user, technical, and administrative.

To address user services, public librarians conduct all kinds of research. In a single hour, a family history buff may ask how to research the Mormon genealogy records, a novelist may need to search newspaper archives regarding an unsolved crime, and an eight-year-old may need help finding the *Ranger Rick* magazine with the article about owls to use in his school report. Most librarians field multiple research questions every day, which are asked in person, by phone, or through e-mail or even text message.

Librarians also develop programs to bring more people into the library. Many libraries conduct children's story hours, so that parents can bring their children for extra reading time. Librarians may also hold programs for seniors, people who are searching for employment, special research groups, groups that need technology training, and even book clubs. The librarian may conduct these meetings or schedule space for others to conduct them. The librarian also schedules special programs according to

GET STARTED NOW!

- In School: College prep, literature, English.
- After School: Volunteer in your school library. Reshelf books, create new entries into the card catalog, and conduct research for other students.
- Around Town: Check out the online resources available at your public library.

what's on the calendar: You may find elementary book clubs during summertime, or special readings built around Banned Books Week during the fall. More and more, librarians turn to blogging, interactive media, and other means of social networking to promote library books and programs.

On the technical services side, librarians choose books, magazines, newspapers, music CDs, videos and DVDs, and other materials for their customers. Librarians must catalog (enter into the card catalog and the library computer system) all new library materials in a consistent manner. They may prepare annotated bibliographies: brief summaries of recommended books and materials that are designed to reinforce library-sponsored lectures or classes. For example, if a librarian sponsors a teen program on graphic novels, he might include an annotated list of criticism and relevant Web sites. Often librarians troubleshoot hardware and software problems and prioritize purchases in these areas. And yes, they still check out, check in, reshelf, and repair books and materials, and they will still send overdue notices.

On the administrative side, librarians are the executive managers of the library. They oversee the management and planning of libraries, negotiate service contracts, materials, and equipment; supervise library employees; perform public relations and fundraising duties; prepare budgets; and direct activities to ensure that everything functions properly.

Clearly librarians have come a long way. They are sleuths, techies, programmers, troubleshooters, communicators, teachers, and masters of the library domain. A love of books is a great start, but you also need to love the people who read them, too.

School Media Specialist

In the olden days the library was where you went when you needed to borrow a book, and the librarian was there to stamp your book and (maybe) tell you to be quiet. In the age of multimedia, where students like you can look up almost anything on a computer (and on your smart phones!) in seconds, almost everything about the school librarian's job has changed—including the title.

Today's school medial specialist is a real part of the school's educational team. Whole classes visit the media center (formerly known as the library) to learn how to get information from books, magazines, newspapers, journals, and online resources. They also learn how to evaluate the quality of this information and integrate it into their schoolwork. Your school media specialist may introduce you to journals that contain valuable information about research topics, or may show you how to find original source material that is archived online. The media specialist is also certainly able to help you find answers to research questions by pointing you in the right direction.

School media specialists must be familiar with the content objectives of each grade level and subject area so that they can assemble appropriate materials and reference sources, and can develop educational goals and select technological tools, like hardware and software, as needed. School media specialists recommend books, magazines, print and online subscriptions, and

GET STARTED NOW!

- In School: College prep, literature, English.
- After School: Volunteer in your school library, or ask if you can use time in there for elective credit.
- Around Town: Visit a school library in an elementary school and in a middle school. Ask the librarians how their jobs have changed in the past few years.

reference materials for purchase by the school media center. They may also advise schools on selecting classroom textbooks and videos, as well as materials for teacher training. With so much money at stake in the face of frequent budget shortfalls, school media specialists must read reviews for textbooks, books, technology, and other materials, and carefully match their orders to school needs. School media specialists also develop policies and procedures regarding the school's responsibility for filtering objectionable material, and access to online sources.

The American Association of School Librarians Web site makes this statement in their "What Parents Should Know" section: "Learning today means more than memorizing facts. It means learning to learn...Savvy parents and educators know that the school library media center is key to teaching students not just to read but to practice the skills they need to seek, evaluate and use information throughout their lives." This statement is a tall order for media center specialists. As they work with teachers and students to prepare reports and tailor learning to students' needs, they also shoulder the responsibility of teaching students how to be inquisitive and then to find the answers they need, both in school and in life.

School Nurse

It's a typical day in the school nurse's office. You have three students quarantined—they have a stomach virus and are waiting for their parents to come. (Yuck.) You just called the parents of a student who has probably broken his wrist in gym class. (Ouch.) After school, you will talk to the football team about avoiding steroid use. (Danger!) As the school nurse, you strive to keep students as healthy and safe as possible.

Many students recall school nurses as the kindest people in their schools. School nurses care for sick and injured students until they can hand them off to their parents, if necessary. It is still just as important that they are compassionate and enjoy interacting with students. They must carefully observe changes in behavior or appearance that may be signs of student health issues.

Today's school nurses are part of schools' overall education teams. They must be well educated in health information and nursing techniques, as well as good administrators who order supplies promptly and run the overall health management of the school. They must also stay current on health trends and new ways of handling existing issues for students and staff at the school. They must be creative teachers, bringing their messages

GET STARTED NOW!

- In School: College prep, biology, chemistry, anatomy, math, health, nutrition.
- After School: Take first-aid and CPR classes to better your lifesaving skills.
- Around Town: Volunteer at a Red Cross blood drive or a public health screening to get a sense of how nurses treat their patients.

into the classroom, and clear communicators, serving as intermediaries among children, parents, and doctors.

Depending on community needs, school nurses might teach elementary and middle school classes on topics like basic hygiene, nutrition, and safety; and high school classes on subjects such as pregnancy prevention, STDs, and child care. The school nurse is also responsible for educating teachers, administrators, and even parents, on things like proper procedure for students who may need EpiPens (an epinephrine injection) for severe allergic reactions, or insulin shots for diabetes, as well as health-related news like flu outbreaks.

School nurses may also assist students who have special needs, and may even help develop Individualized Education Plans (IEPs) for these students. Teachers may need to learn how to handle different medical situations as these students are mainstreamed into classrooms of typical students.

School nurses also screen for all kinds of illnesses and ailments—nurses can screen for anything from head lice to sickle-cell anemia. They can spot medical disorders, child-abuse injuries, and developmental issues, and help teachers determine what course to follow. The school nurse sets school policy for these issues, and may also help administrators develop emergency plans for everything from lockdowns and national security alerts to natural disaster procedures.

Nursing is a high-demand profession with many opportunities all over the country and the world. School nurses have the reputation for being calm in emergencies and kind when students need comfort. If you want to combine health care with teaching and administration, then nursing in a school offers everything you need.

School Psychologist

A school psychologist has some responsibilities that are similar to those of a guidance counselor or school social worker. So how are they different? School psychologists have more training in psychology, which means they are specifically equipped to handle situations involving students with identified disabilities or with psychological challenges. They can administer and interpret psycho-educational tests to determine whether a student is eligible for special education services. School psychologists are well educated in learning theory, child development, and mental health and behavior in the school environment.

As a school psychologist, you would often work with students who have been referred by teachers for a variety of reasons. One student might be referred because he has difficulty completing assignments, and is falling behind in class. After assessing for dyslexia and for depression with negative results, you take the student to the school nurse for an eye exam. Sure enough, the student has trouble seeing examples and copying assignments that are written on the board. You refer his parents to an ophthalmologist, and also help his teacher develop a tutoring program that will help him catch up. When doctors determine that this student's vision loss is extreme and irreversible, you refer him for special services

GET STARTED NOW!

- In School: Psychology and child development.
- After School: Volunteer for any school groups that involve tutoring or mentoring, mediation, and support.
- Around Town: Volunteer to work with on organization that deals with children. For example, volunteer at a group home or orphanage, or for a school that teaches students with special needs.

CAREER 411

Search It!
Try the American Psychological Association at http://www.apa.org/index.aspx and the National Association of School Psychologists at http://www.nasponline.org/about_sp/whatis.aspx.

Surf It!
Find out how a real school psychologist answers tough questions. Browse topics on the School Psychology Blog at http://www.schoolpsychologyblog.com.

Read It!
Catch the latest school psychology news at http://www.schoolpsychology.net.

Learn It!
Minimum Education: Master's degree.

Typical Majors: Psychology, educational psychology, child psychology.

Special Skills: Desire to help others, excellent problem-solving skills, active listening skills, integrity, discretion, cooperation, stress tolerance, leadership.

Earn It!
Median annual salary is $66,040.

(Source: U.S. Department of Labor)

for visually impaired students. He gets the extra help he needs to succeed at school and to cope with his vision loss.

School psychologists work with students of all ages. They may assess preschoolers to determine where they should be placed. They work with teachers and parents to teach them to help elementary school children cope with developmental delays, or to deal with anxiety or control impulsive behavior. In upper grades, school psychologists play important roles in identifying students who are dealing with depression, thoughts of suicide, substance abuse, truancy, family problems, and even pregnancy. While psychologists may work directly with students to resolve these problems, they may also refer them to outside services, since it is not uncommon for one psychologist to be assigned to more than 1,000 students.

In the aftermath of a traumatic event, such as a natural disaster, death of a teacher or of a student, or school violence, school psychologists may play a special role in helping others cope. They may provide workshops for dealing with fear or grief. They can also provide classes on special subjects like bullying, substance abuse, gang activity, or pregnancy prevention, as needed.

IF YOU WERE. . .

As a school psychologist for a middle school, how would you handle the school bully?

. . . MAKE IT REAL!

Start by gathering background information from resources like the American Psychological Association at http://www.apa.org/topics/bullying/index.aspx and http://www.apa.org/news/press/releases/2010/04/bullying.aspx. Prepare a list of 10 interview questions to ask the child, and a second list of 10 suggestions for him to follow if he is to remain in school without further disciplinary action.

School psychologists must be mature, stable, and objective when dealing with students. It can be an emotional career choice since your services are often required when students are facing crisis and heartache. But, following a school psychologist's suggestions is often one of the first, important steps for students to improve, recover, and heal.

School Social Worker

Your clients are students, but they have other issues besides learning. Some of them come to school on Monday morning without having eaten since free school lunch on Friday. Some spend the weekend trying to avoid abuse. Some of them spent most of Saturday in the care of a sibling instead of a parent, because mom has left the home and dad had to work all day. Some struggled with homework all weekend because no one else in the home can read well enough to help. Most people think of school as a place to learn, but thanks to school social workers, it can also be a place to get help.

School social workers are the link between students' lives at home, at school, and within the community. Because of their training and their contact with students and their teachers, school social workers may be among the first ones to notice behavioral changes caused by substance abuse, physical or sexual abuse, an increase in poverty, failing family dynamics, or other situations that are often out of students' control. When a school social worker believes a serious problem exists, he or she may talk to the family at school, or conduct a home visit.

GET STARTED NOW!

- In School: College prep, child development, sociology, psychology.
- After School: Become a peer counselor at your school. Or volunteer to be a big buddy to some younger students.
- Around Town: Look for opportunities to serve members of your community. Work at a soup kitchen or build houses for a charity organization.

When a school social worker meets with a family, the first order of business is assessing the situation; if the child is in danger, a social worker will work to remove the child from the home. If the child is not in danger, the school social worker will help parents understand how to better attend to a child's needs, and may refer them to an outside government or medical agency, school program, or social service resource that will help them understand those needs. School social workers often set up support groups for students with similar needs, such as divorcing parents or abuse in the home. If any students have difficulty behaving in school, school social workers help teachers and administrators develop strategies for working with these students, using their knowledge of the students' backgrounds—the "bigger picture"— to help teachers understand the cultural, economic, family, and health issues that contribute to the student's behavior.

School social workers may be a part of the team that determines an Individualized Education Plan (IEP), an action plan that determines teaching strategies for students with learning disabilities, and follow up on making sure the school is following laws and correctly filling out paperwork for these students. They may also help integrate students with special needs into the regular school population.

Thanks to growing populations, an emphasis on integrating students with special needs into mainstream classrooms, and a continuing occurrence of problematic social issues, the need for school social workers is likely to increase. Availability of state and local funding, however, will ultimately dictate the actual job growth.

Secondary School Teacher

Your students have finished reading *The Scarlet Letter* by Nathaniel Hawthorne, and are making videos of crucial scenes. One year, the entire class handed out red candy in every scene to emphasize the color's symbolism. Another year, two students mimed the meeting in the forest by using space-age music. Students think that making these videos is incredibly silly, but they read their assigned scenes carefully and usually incorporate clever ideas. This project takes up plenty of class time but students enjoy it and know the material afterward. That's why you go the extra mile to have them work on it.

Secondary school teachers, like the English teacher described above, must be experts in the subjects they teach. They also must be creative motivators who get students excited about (or even just tolerant of) the subjects. They search for creative ways to make the subject exciting while being realistic about what students can do at each grade level, without making it too easy (boring) or too challenging (frustrating).

There is much more to teaching than standing in front of class after class. Teachers must attend continuing education classes to stay current on teaching methods and developments in the subject

CAREER 411

Search It!
American Federation of Teachers at http://www.aft.org and National Education Association at http://www.nea.org.

Surf It!
Play this virtual high school game if you need a reminder: http://www.games2win.com/en/adventure/play-a_day_at_high_school.asp.

Read It!
Check out Web sites for the subject area you are interested in, such as English (http://www.ncte.org), mathematics (http://www.nctm.org), science (http://www.nsta.org), social studies (http://www.socialstudies.org), and technology, (http://www.iste.org/welcome.aspx).

Learn It!
Minimum Education: Bachelor's degree, plus student teaching experience and state certification.

Typical Majors: Major in the subject area you would like to teach.

Special Skills: Patience, creativity, active listening, organization skills, communication skills, integrity, ability to handle stress.

Earn It!
Median annual salary is $52,200.

(Source: U.S. Department of Labor)

GET STARTED NOW!

- In School: Take as many classes as possible in the subject you would like to teach. Choose your favorite—that is the one you are likely to be good at teaching.
- After School: Join your school's chapter of Future Educators of America (http://www.futureeducators.org).
- Around Town: Consider teaching a children's class at your favorite place of worship or recreation.

area, as well as on changes in state standards. (These are often scheduled during breaks and summer vacation!) There is also a lot of planning involved. Teachers must explain the information as they create projects and lessons that help students learn in a variety of ways. Students may learn by listening, doing, writing, or by discussing what they have read or seen. Lessons containing each of these components will reach more students, and be more fun.

Teachers also grade assignments, fill out progress reports, meet with parents, tutor students, write college recommendations, participate in committees, and often coach a sport or run an extracurricular activity. As they carry out other responsibilities, they think about how to best teach each one of hundreds of students. The sheer volume of work expected from secondary teachers is daunting. Imagine grading 300 algebra tests or social studies reports.

Many teachers start working hours before school begins and leave long after the school day is over.

Teachers work in many different kinds of high schools. There are public schools, private schools, religious schools, and magnet or career schools that focus on a particular set of skills or talents. There are also "alternative schools," set up for students who have difficulty, for whatever reason, succeeding in a regular school. If you are an expert in your subject and know how to reach students, any of these might be a good fit. Hopefully, regardless of the subject you teach and the type of high school you choose, you will become that teacher your students remember fondly after they graduate.

Special Education Teacher

CAREER 411

Search It!
National Association of Special Education Teachers at http://www.naset.org.

Surf It!
Find answers to important questions about special needs for general educators at http://serge.ccsso.org/essential_questions.html.

Read It!
Peruse resources used by special needs teachers at http://www.teachervision.fen.com/special-education/teacher-resources/6640.html/.

Learn It!
Minimum Education: Bachelor's degree, plus state licensure.

Typical Majors: Special education.

Special Skills: Patience, flexibility, stress tolerance, cooperation, dependability, integrity, persistence, excellent organizational skills.

Earn It!
Median annual salary is $51,940.

(Source: U.S. Department of Labor)

Your class is always very quiet, but everyone is always moving. In your classroom for hearing impaired students, your students communicate with their hands. As you turn your back to write on the blackboard, you can hear two students signing a lively discussion instead of paying attention to the lesson. As you turn to face them, all hands stop at once! That's progress—they are getting better at signing and at socializing. Your job is to teach these elementary students academics and signing, and prepare them for a regular classroom environment, so socializing is good.

Pursuing a career in special education gives teachers the opportunity to develop meaningful relationships with students who may have any variety of disabilities. Early intervention is the most effective way to reach these students, which is why special ed teachers may work with infants and toddlers in their homes. Special education can continue all the way through high school, depending on students' needs and capabilities.

Although schools have traditionally placed students with disabilities in self-contained classrooms, the current trend is to work toward "mainstreaming" students as soon as possible, if assistance is necessary. Although there may be different expectations for the child with special needs, the goal is for that child to benefit from the exposure to peers who are on target developmentally.

GET STARTED NOW!

- In School: College prep, child and developmental psychology.
- After School: Volunteer to tutor students with disabilities.
- Around Town: Spend some time at a hospital or other facility for children with disabilities.

When schools follow inclusion policies, there is still plenty of work for special education teachers! They may assist students in the inclusion classroom by acting as "shadows," providing help with daily tasks. They also work with classroom teachers to modify lessons and adapt curriculum to make it more appropriate for the student. They may also work in resource rooms: special areas where small groups or individuals come for part of the day, if full-day inclusion is not ideal. During the workday it is often the special education teacher's job to evaluate students and determine their needs. There is also a great deal of paperwork and monitoring required to establish and carry out a student's IEP (individualized education plan), as well as to make sure that all actions regarding each student are legally compliant.

Special education teachers see great progress in their students. It is highly rewarding to help a nonverbal student speak or write for the first time, assist a student with autism to make eye contact, teach a student with severe ADHD how to cope with longer assignments, or watch a student with disabilities make friends with classmates. While their progress may be slower than that of other students, their accomplishments are tremendous to watch.

Speech-Language Pathologist

People just automatically learn to talk correctly, correct? Once you learn how to talk, you never forget, right? The answer to both questions is, "Not necessarily." Some children have difficulty speaking. Strokes and other issues associated with accidents, disease, or aging can rob people of their ability to speak. A speech-language pathologist (SLP) helps with these problems.

Speech is the ability to make recognizable communication using breathing, vocalizations, and pauses. Language is the ability to communicate through a shared set of rules, such as putting words in the "right" order and using correct words to name objects. Difficulty with these skills can come from poor muscle control, learning disabilities, physical disabilities, stroke, or other diseases or disorders. SLPs diagnose and treat problems with oral communication, and with swallowing.

SLPs play a critical role in schools. They screen children for delayed language and speech disorders. An SLP diagnoses and treats children with a range of difficulties. For example, you might help a child with selective mutism by helping her parents identify situations that cause her to choose not to speak. You may help a

GET STARTED NOW!

- In School: College prep, foreign language, linguistics.
- After School: Ask your school guidance counselor to arrange for you to interview your school district's SLP to find out about the job experience.
- Around Town: Volunteer to help during a school or community hearing screening day.

CAREER 411

Search It!
The American Speech-Language-Hearing Association at http://www.asha.org and National Student Speech Language Hearing Association at http://www.nsslha.org.

Surf It!
Watch a video interview of an SLP at http://www.dailymotion.com/video/xf1593_speech-development-in-children_people.

Read It!
Check out a quick guide to common language problems at TeensHealth at http://kidshealth.org/teen/diseases_conditions/sight/speech_disorders.html or visit the National Aphasia Association at http://www.aphasia.org.

Learn It!
Minimum Education: Master's degree for most states, plus licensure.

Typical Majors: Linguistics, speech-language pathology, audiology.

Special Skills: Patience, research skills, flexibility, social perceptiveness, excellent communication skills, problem-solving skills.

Earn It!
Median annual salary is $65,090.
(Source: U.S. Department of Labor)

child with dyslexia who is having trouble with comprehension and reading aloud by teaching him how to summarize. A preschooler who cannot say the "r" sound needs help learning to form it in her mouth. A client with Down Syndrome may need therapy for a swallowing difficulty. You frequently work as part of a team of teachers, parents, psychologists, and physicians. You may also travel between schools or to client's homes.

Your services are important to older people, too. Speech-language pathologists provide therapy for aphasia (loss of speech and language capabilities) or for swallowing difficulties caused by stroke, brain trauma, or cancer. Your job is to assist them as they regain their abilities to communicate. If speech is not possible, you may find a device, such as a computer, that replaces a client's voice.

Some SLPs specialize in business communications, including helping clients modify a foreign or regional accent, especially in cases where the accent, rather than the speaker's meaning, becomes a negative focus of people's attention. SLPs train people who frequently make presentations, helping them effectively speak and use gestures, facial expressions, and body postures to communicate.

As a speech-language pathologist in an elementary school, how would you help a student with a stutter?

. . . MAKE IT REAL!

Do some online research on stuttering. Find resources at the Stuttering Foundation (http://www.stuttersfa.org) and the National Stuttering Association (http://www.nsastutter.org). Then find five activities to use with the student. Create a written lesson plan that outlines how to incorporate each activity into your first therapy session.

In all cases, SLPs must understand clients' cultural, verbal, and nonverbal traditions. For example, in some cultures, children traditionally address adults in low voices and avoid eye contact. An SLPs should be able to differentiate between a true disability and this type of cultural norm.

The need for SLPs is expected to grow faster than average, according to the U.S. Department of Labor. This is partly due to the aging population and to medical advances that save the lives of stroke victims and premature infants. It is a good time to enter this profession.

Student Affairs Officer

Higher education can be challenging for students to navigate. Whom do you ask about getting a grade changed, or double majoring, or applying for financial aid, or whether or not your community college courses will transfer? Student affairs professionals help students find answers. There are many different student affairs positions—no two are exactly alike. Their major functions can be summarized, however, as providing counseling, management, and administration for all aspects of campus life outside of the classroom. Specialized functions may include any of the following.

Admissions counselors recruit students who best fit at an institution, then evaluate applications and decide whom to admit. Some schools employ enrollment managers who identify applicants most likely to graduate from the school rather than drop out, leave to play professional sports, or transfer. Higher level admissions counselors can recommend undergraduates for specific departments or schools within the institution, such as architecture or pre-law.

Campus activities and student organization specialists provide opportunities for students to develop leadership skills through student organizations. They may also oversee a university's Greek system.

GET STARTED NOW!

- In School: College prep, public speaking, communications.
- After School: Get involved in campus life at your school: Make props for a school play, join a service club, or help out during freshmen orientation events.
- Around Town: Visit the office of student affairs online or in person at a local college.

Financial aid counselors have expert knowledge of federal, state, and local regulations and aid programs. They recommend strategies for obtaining financial aid and help students assemble aid packages. They may also seek out employment for students on financial aid.

Student career counselors assist students in choosing career paths. They administer career and personality tests, help students find part-time or summer employment or internships, and arrange for on-campus career days. There are also regular student counselors who help students with personal or academic problems.

General directors of student affairs may handle more complex issues, such as advising students and faculty on degree completion requirements. They identify students with GPA or progress issues, can be responsible for placing students on academic probation, and advise them on how to improve their academic standing. Directors may help students resolve academic grievances. They can also help students plan interdisciplinary programs, double majors, and work-study programs.

Residence life staff members deal with residence plans and policies, such as housing freshmen, conducting residence hall lotteries for upperclassmen, and providing student leadership on a daily basis. They also set policies governing campus residence facilities.

Other student affairs professionals oversee new student orientation, the student union, and student advocacy. Student orientation programs help new students succeed socially and academically. Many schools offer orientation programs the summer before students' freshman year. Student union professionals make and implement decisions about facilities, retail services, and hiring outside speakers or performers. Student advocacy professionals support and advocate for specific groups of students, such as students with disabilities or international students.

Since student affairs officers set the tone for most aspects of campus life, they must conduct themselves impeccably. They must also keep in mind what it was that made college so great—and keep doing that as much as possible (within the rules, of course).

Technology Administrator

When evaluating prospective schools, parents and students often lead with this question: "What technology is available?" Plenty of professions and businesses now require technology skills, especially as they modernize their computers and servers, and deal with the implications of social media. Since people are more likely to be comfortable with technology when exposed to it at an early age, educational institutions are increasingly likely to have technology administrators.

Technology administrators provide two basic types of services to schools. First, on a local scale, technology administrators offer services to students and teachers. As a school technology administrator, you know what students need to know about computers. You might even teach computer lab during classes. You might research age-appropriate skill-based and research Web sites. And you advise teachers on using technology to enhance other subjects, and on the subject of technology itself. It is also your responsibility to choose software and hardware for the school while staying within budget.

Some technology administrators work on a larger scale to oversee computer and server operations for their school, district, or campus. As a school district technology administrator, you might be asked to explore new server options for the district, trouble-

GET STARTED NOW!

- In School: Take all the computer classes your schedule will allow.
- After School: Join the school computer club.
- Around Town: Ask to interview someone from the IT department at a local vocational school or university and see if you can "shadow" them for a day on the job.

CAREER 411

Search It!
The Association for Educational Communications and Technology at http://www.aect.org.

Surf It!
Catch up with the latest news at the Consortium of School Networking at http://www.cosn.org.

Read It!
Explore school technology trends at http://www.edtechmag.com.

Learn It!
Minimum Education: Bachelor's or master's degree.

Typical Majors: Computer science, school administration, information systems, network administration.

Special Skills: Excellent computer skills, research skills, communication skills, problem-solving skills, teaching and leadership skills, persistence.

Earn It!
Median annual salary is $112,210.
(Source: U.S. Department of Labor)

shoot Internet connection problems at a high school, provide a training session on the new electronic grade-reporting system for all school administrators, or train new middle school teachers to create their own classroom Web sites. For a university you might be asked to outsource Internet connection installation in a new dorm; research and upgrade software; track down the person who is sending obscene e-mails to the biochemistry professor; increase the server's storage capacity for electronic student records; or help the mathematics department implement new, online, distance learning courses. You might also be responsible for teaching technology courses, especially in vocational schools or programs that specialize in IT management.

This job description varies widely depending on the institution. Perhaps the most important word in this job description is "troubleshooting." Technology is constantly changing as software upgrades come out, processors run faster, remote learning becomes more popular, memory needs increase, and new products are introduced to the market. Keeping up with innovations

IF YOU WERE...

A technology administrator for your high school and the principal asked you to recommend the best ways to use technology in school, what would your ideal classroom look like?

...MAKE IT REAL!

Visit the "Re-imagining Learning in the 21st Century" section of the McArthur Foundation Web site (http://www.macfound.org/site/c.lkLXJ8MQKrH/b.5796441/k.D62D/ReImagining_Learning_in_the_21st_Century.htm) for ideas about how some of the ways students currently use technology socially could be effective in classroom situations. Then sketch out your best suggestions for a totally wired 21st-century classroom.

so that your institution is current and competitive is a form of troubleshooting, too.

There are many corporate jobs for technology administrators, as well. They do the same things for businesses as they do for schools: train employees on new software, order and maintain hardware, run servers, administer Web sites, budget for upgrades, and troubleshoot any problems for management and employees.

Learning institutions and businesses are so dependent on technology now that when anything goes wrong, as it often does with sensitive systems, technology administrators have to get things running again, often with impatient users breathing down their necks. While "The system is down!" are words you dread hearing, there is power in knowing you can be the one to fix it.

Textbook Publisher

May is busy. First you head to the International Reading Association (IRA) convention to represent your publishing company. You attend sessions, brainstorm with your product developers after their sessions, meet a new author, and walk the convention floor. Back in the office, you sign off on a new social studies textbook and teachers' guide, brainstorm a publishing list with the editorial and product development departments, meet with your textbook adoption committee, and host a supplemental software publisher who wants to collaborate on online student math games that will dovetail with an upcoming elementary textbook. At the end of the month you're off to New York for BookExpo.

Textbook publishing involves managing people who conduct research, reinvent the wheel, innovate, do guesswork, and look for needles in the haystack. First in the process of publishing a new textbook, your staff does research: on what other publishers are up to, about state and university curriculum standards and course offerings, about what different consumer groups think about current textbook content, and about standardized test changes. All of this affects your textbook's content.

Reinventing the wheel means offering what all other textbook publishers offer—but better. You must include standard content or your textbook will be ignored because it leaves things out. But even though you reinvent the wheel, if you can find a unique way to present the information, then you can innovate. Maybe the art-

GET STARTED NOW!

- In School: College prep, creative writing, English.
- After School: Evaluate your textbooks. What do you like and dislike about them?
- Around Town: Go online and investigate e-textbooks and consider this new wave of digital innovation.

work is exceptional, or the writing style is particularly appealing, or your textbook explains things clearly. Making standout products increases the textbook's chances for adoption by universities or school districts.

Once you reinvent the wheel and innovate, the next step is to guess. At IRA and BookExpo sessions you find out what educators, administrators, the Department of Education, and others are talking about. What's the next big thing in math? How will high schools combine technology with science? Will physics professors lecture about the Large Hadron Collider? In textbook publishing it's best to be like the surfer riding the crest of the next big educational trend wave, so that schools adopt your textbook first, before too many others crowd the market in your wake.

Finally, once you decide on the parameters of your textbook, it's time to find that needle in a haystack—that author or team of authors who, ideally, is well known in the field for being both innovative and grounded in the basics, who identifies with your vision, and who is willing to complete the textbook and add their stamp of approval. Once you find all of these things, you set the wheels in motion and check that textbook off of your list until review time. Now on to planning the next one.

Tutor

Has there ever been a time when you struggled with schoolwork? Maybe that Honors Algebra II class moved just a little too fast. Or there was that time you waited until the day before the event to start your science fair project. Every student faces some academic bumps in the road, but for some students, things spiral out of control. Teachers usually make sure that students use skills they have already learned to help them master new ones. If you have trouble mastering a skill, then you cannot use it to learn other skills. Once you fall behind, you are missing something that you need to move on. Tutors are there to fill in gaps in learning and help students master skills they need to keep moving ahead.

There are many ways to be a professional tutor. Some tutors are teachers who decide to tutor privately. They meet with individual students or small groups to do additional work on skills. In this environment, students can ask more questions and get more one-on-one help. They can work on material they have already covered, or get a preview of what is coming up, so that class time itself will be a review. As a private tutor, you can set your own hours, and you can get referrals from local schools, so you can work with those teachers and know what they are covering at the time.

Tutors can also work for companies that specialize in tutoring. These companies usually have local franchises in different

GET STARTED NOW!

- **In School:** Take college prep and load up electives in subject areas of particular interest.
- **After School:** Volunteer as a tutor with peers at your own school or with younger students in an after-school enrichment program.
- **Around Town:** Ask to visit a local tutoring center and interview one of the tutors. Find out what the job entails.

IF YOU WERE. . .

As a test prep tutor, how would you help students score well on the SATs?

. . . MAKE IT REAL!

Do an Internet search for free SAT advice, such as the advice found at http://www.testinfo.net/sat/sat-tips.htm. Use the ideas and strategies you discover to create a SAT prep calendar for students, offering one short exercise to do or a tip to think about every other night.

communities. Tutors who work for franchises often perform diagnostic tests to see where students' learning deficiencies are in the subject areas for which the students request help. The tutors prepare an individualized learning plan for each student, and then set up a schedule to meet with the student, usually on a weekly basis. Tutoring centers usually use regular school hours for paperwork and save nights and weekends for meeting with students.

Tutors work on all levels and with all kinds of subjects. You could tutor college students at the university writing center, or you could work with elementary students who have dyslexia or other learning disabilities, or you could work with adult ESL students who are trying to learn English language and culture. Tutors also help with college test prep courses. They can tutor students on intangible things like study skills and time management. And tutoring does not always have to happen face-to-face, since online tutoring resources are now available.

Tutoring can be very rewarding as you give students that one-on-one contact teachers always say they wish they had enough time for. It feels wonderful to watch a student go from being frustrated to having confidence and success. Sometimes a little progress is all that is needed to remind students that they can succeed if they just get a little help.

Vocational and Technical Education Instructor

CAREER 411

Search It!

The Association for Career and Technical Education at http://www.acteonline.org.

Surf It!

Visit the *Dirty Jobs* episode guide at http://dsc.discovery.com/fansites/dirtyjobs/episode/episode.html and learn about all kinds of fascinating jobs.

Read It!

Learn the history of community college and look at potential interview questions in this article at http://www.mla.org/commcollege_teachcar.

Learn It!

Minimum Education: Two-year degree in a skilled trade, bachelor's degree, and certification in academic subjects.

Typical Majors: Skilled trades or academic subject areas.

Special Skills: Leadership, expertise in a technical or academic field, desire to help people, communication skills, organizational skills, critical-thinking skills, dependability, problem-solving skills.

Earn It!

Median annual salary is $49,950.

(Source: U.S. Department of Labor)

As a plumbing instructor, your job is to teach students the proper materials, tools, and installation techniques to use when building or modifying any plumbing system. It is an important job. People depend on plumbers to keep houses and neighborhoods sanitary and to provide clean water. This skill set is very specific, and requires training and certification, since an untrained plumber can ruin a home. Vocational and technical education prepares students for highly skilled occupations that require specific training. Plumbers, as well as aircraft pilots, computer programmers, dieticians, graphic artists, ultrasound technicians, welders, and other skilled workers learn their trades from vocational and technical instructors.

Vocational and technical education is more than just learning skills for a specific job. It also involves linking traditional academic subject matter (language arts, math, science, social studies) to a

GET STARTED NOW!

- In School: Find out if your school district partners with a local technical or community college to provide vocational and technical education. Sign up for a course that interests you.
- After School: Consider joining career-focused school clubs like Family, Career and Community Leaders of America (http://www.fcclainc.org), or DECA (http://www.deca.org).
- Around Town: Look into joining a local chapter of SkillsUSA at http://www.skillsusa.org, a group for teachers, students, and employers of trade and technical professions.

real-world context. Vocational and technical students also learn other job-related skills like responsibility and workplace ethics.

Vocational instructors may teach in middle schools or high schools, magnet schools, career centers, or community colleges or technical schools. In middle schools, instructors introduce students to a wide variety of career fields. High school students mix work-based activities with classroom learning. Vocational schools also retrain unemployed adults for new careers. Adults may participate in welfare-to-work programs, and upgrade current career skills. Many technical schools also provide courses in personal enrichment. Adults can take foreign languages, culinary classes, fitness and heath, and self-help courses.

Vocational and technical instructors have the benefit of working with local employers who may help them tailor courses to company needs, and in turn, offer student internships or work-studies. At the postsecondary level these connections help educators provide training for local jobs. Classes offer hands-on experience in real-life settings to show students what to expect from future work environments. For example, plumbers may take students to construction sites, let them watch workers use tools and equipment to fit pipes, and have them repeat pipe-fitting and other procedures until they meet the trade's specific standards.

At all school levels vocational and technical educators have the same responsibilities to their degree-earning students as any other high school or college teachers. They prepare and administer lessons, manage the classroom, grade assignments, attend faculty meetings, and keep abreast of developments in their fields. They may be responsible for creating and teaching online courses. They also make sure they provide courses that will train workers to work for local businesses. Community colleges can be key to attracting new businesses to an area.

Vocational and technical teachers help students meet challenges in the workforce. With their unique combination of academic courses and skills training, community colleges ensure that students succeed in traditional college courses, have excellent technical skills, and will thrive in a professional environment.

EXPERIMENT WITH SUCCESS

Stop! Hold it right there. You are so not ready to experiment with success until you have explored your way to a career idea that makes you wonder, "Is this one right for me?"

You will know you are ready to take things to the next level when you are still curious about a specific career idea even after you have used the tools featured in Section Two to:

- Investigate that career idea so thoroughly that you know almost as much about what it's like as someone who is already doing it
- Complete a Hire Yourself activity with impressive results

If, after all that, you still want to know more, this section is where you can crank things up by:

- Talking with people who already have careers like the one you want
- Looking at different types of employment situations where people get paid to do what you want to do
- Figuring out a few next steps for getting from where you are now (high school) to where you want to go (a successful career)

In other words, you are going to:

- ASK for advice and start building a career-boosting network
- ASSESS a variety of workplace options
- ADDRESS options to make the most of now to get ready for a successful future

ASK for Advice and Start Building a Career-Boosting Network

There's nothing like going straight to the source to find out what a specific career is really like. After all, who's more likely to have the inside scoop on the real deal than someone who has actually "been there, done that." It is surprisingly easy to get most people talking about their careers. All you have to do is ask.

E-mail, Twitter, Facebook, and other cool social networking tools now make it easier than ever to touch base with almost any expert in the world for advice and information. But whether you conduct your career chats the old-fashioned way with face-to-face conversations or via the latest and greatest technologies, the following tips will help you make a good first impression.

1 **Practice with people you already know.** Start asking parents, relatives, neighbors, and other trusted adults to talk about what their work is really like, and you're likely to be amazed by what you find out.

2 **Think about what you want to know before you start asking questions.** Jot down a few questions that you can refer to if you get nervous or the conversation starts to lag. Keep the conversation flowing by asking open-ended questions that require more than simple yes or no answers like:

- Tell me about...
- How do you feel about...?
- What was it like...?

3 **Be polite, professional, and considerate of the person's time.** In other words, don't be a pest! Just because you can access any person, any place, any time doesn't mean that you should.

4 **Seek answers *and* advice.** Make the most of any opportunity to learn from other people's successes and mistakes. Be sure to ask them what they know now that they wish they had known when they were your age.

You may want to add some of these questions to your interviews:

- How do your childhood interests relate to your choice of career path?
- How did you first learn about the job you have today?
- In what ways is your job different from how you expected it to be?
- What is a typical day on the job like for you?
- What are the best and worst parts of your job?

- If anything were possible, how would you change your job description?
- What kinds of people do you usually meet in your work?
- How is your product made (or service delivered)?
- What other kinds of professionals work here?
- Tell me about the changes you have seen in your industry over the years. What do you see as the future of the industry?

5 **Keep your career-information network growing.**
Conclude each interview with a sincere thank you and a request for recommendations about other people or resources to turn to for additional information.

CAREER CHATS

Think about who knows what you want to know. Use online news and professional association Web sites to identify experts in your field of interest. For extra help finding contact information, use Google to identify the person's company Web site or other professional affiliations. And, of course, do make use of the time-honored "friend of a friend of a friend" network to find contacts known to friends, parents, neighbors, teachers, and others who share an interest in helping you succeed.

Depending on each person's availability, interviews can be arranged onsite at a person's place of employment (with parental permission and supervision only), via a prescheduled phone conversation, or online with e-mail, Skype, or other social networking tools. Find out which method is most convenient for the person you'd like to interview.

One note of encouragement (and caution) before you get started. Most people are more than happy to talk about their careers. After all, who doesn't like talking about themselves? So, on the one hand, you don't have to worry about asking since most people will say yes if they have the time. On the other hand, you'll want to be careful about who you contact. Take every precaution to make sure that every person is legit (as opposed to being certified creepers) and make sure that a trusted adult (such as a parent or teacher) has your back as you venture out into the real world.

With that said, use the following chart (or, if this book does not belong to you, create one like it) to keep track of whom you contact and what they say. Once you get the hang of it, use the same process to contact others who are likely to know what you need to know about your future career.

Contact Information

Name: _____

Company: _____

Title: _____

Company Web Site: _____

Preferred Contact Method: _____

❏ Phone _____

❏ E-mail _____

❏ Twitter _____

❏ Facebook _____

❏ Blog _____

❏ Other _____

CONTACT LOG		
Date/Time	Question	Answer

Lessons Learned

Nice as it is to talk to other people about their success, there's a point where you can't help but wonder what it all means for you. Here's your chance to apply what you've learned from your career chats to your own situation. Take a few minutes to think through your best answers to the following questions:

- What do you know about this career that you didn't know before?
- What kind of knowledge and skills do you need to acquire to prepare for a career like this?
- Are you more or less inclined to pursue this type of career? Why or why not?

ASSESS a Variety of Workplace Options

Employers come in all shapes and sizes. They run the gamut from huge multinational conglomerates to small mom-and-pop shops with a lot of options in-between. Big or small, before any employer agrees to hire you, they are going to want to know pretty much everything there is to know about you. Where did you go to school? What kind of grades did you make? What are your professional goals? Questions like these will keep flying until an employer is absolutely certain that you are the right choice for their company.

But guess what? It takes two to create a mutually beneficial employment relationship—an employer who gets what he needs and an employee who gets what he wants. In other words, that get-acquainted curiosity cuts both ways. It's just as important for you to find out if the company is a good fit for you as it is for them. After all, your success is their success and vice versa.

In most cases it's a bit early to decide on your ultimate employer with any precision. However, it's the perfect time to take a look at the options. Can you see yourself in the fast-paced world of a high-powered Fortune 500 firm? Are you better suited for an energetic, entrepreneurial, start-up company? Would you just as soon shuck the corporate world for a job that lets you work outdoors or, perhaps, one that requires a lot of travel?

Figuring out what kind of environment you want to work in is almost as important as figuring out what you want to do. Fortunately the Internet makes scouting out workplace options just a few mouse clicks away. Use the following tips to find out more about employers who hire people to do the kind of work you want to do.

- **Surf the Web** to seek out companies according to industry, career type, or geographic location. For instance, a quick Google search for "agribusiness" is likely to yield a list of resources that includes the U.S. Department of Agriculture to companies specializing in everything from beverages and beehives to snack foods and seeds.

- **Find a List** that meets some sort of criteria. Want to work for one of the nation's biggest, most successful companies? Run a search for Fortune 500 companies at http://www.forbes.com. Want to find an exciting, up-and-coming company? Look for a list of "fastest growing companies" at http://www.inc.com or http://money.cnn.com. Want to find a company that treats its employees especially well? Track down a list of great places to work at http://www.greatplacestowork.com. Prefer a family-friendly company? Check out Working Mother's lists of bests at http://www.workingmother.com/best-companies.

- **Visit Company Web Sites** to compare opportunities associated with different kinds of employment situations— government, corporate, and small business, for instance. Simply run a search for the name of any company you want to know about—even most small companies have a Web site these days. Be sure to check out the current "careers" or "job listings" sections to get a sense of what the company looks for and offers prospective employees. Also use the Google news feature to look for current newsworthy articles about a prospective employer.

How a company presents itself online offers an interesting perspective of what the company's culture might be like. These types of online resources also offer a great way to find out more about a company's products and services, mission, values, clients, and reputation. The bonus is all the contact names and details you can use to seek out additional information.

Employer Profiles

Ready for a little cyber-snooping? Go online to track down information about three different types of employers: **a major corporation** (think Fortune 500); **a small business** (think entrepreneurial); and **a government agency** (think local, state, or federal) that offers opportunities associated with the career pathway you'd like to pursue. Use the following chart to record your discoveries and compare the results.

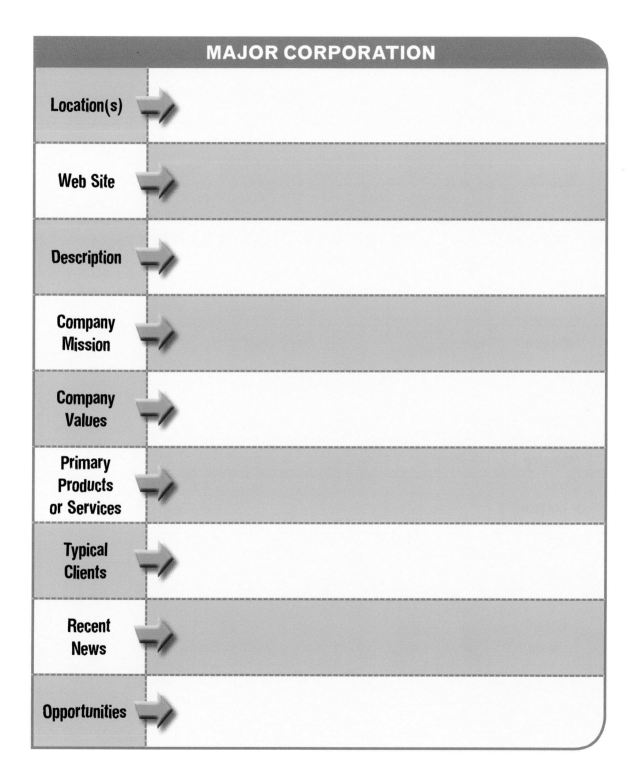

MAJOR CORPORATION

Location(s)	
Web Site	
Description	
Company Mission	
Company Values	
Primary Products or Services	
Typical Clients	
Recent News	
Opportunities	

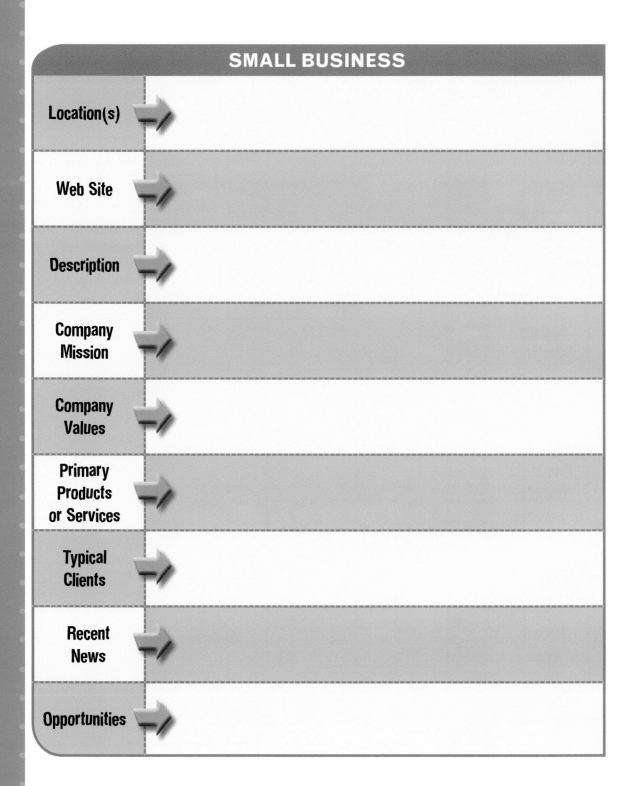

SMALL BUSINESS

Location(s)	
Web Site	
Description	
Company Mission	
Company Values	
Primary Products or Services	
Typical Clients	
Recent News	
Opportunities	

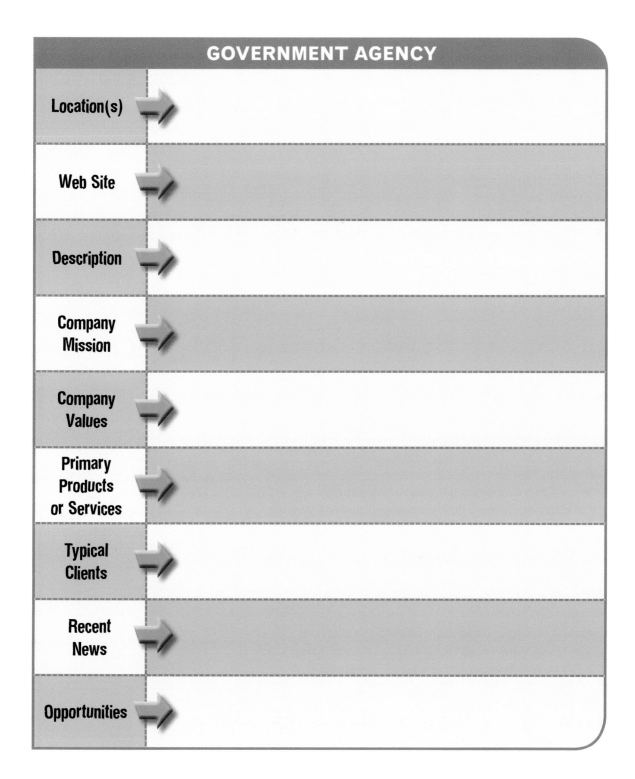

GOVERNMENT AGENCY

Location(s)	
Web Site	
Description	
Company Mission	
Company Values	
Primary Products or Services	
Typical Clients	
Recent News	
Opportunities	

Lessons Learned

Take time out to think through what you've learned about your workplace preferences. Use the following chart to compare the pros and cons of each situation and apply what you learned to what you want in a future work environment.

	Major Corporation
Based on your first impression of the company's Web site, how would you describe each employer?	
What factor(s) did you find most appealing about each company? (Size, geographic location, opportunities for advancement, etc.)	
What factor(s) did you like least about the company?	
What (if any) types of employment opportunities interested you most at each company?	
In what ways does (or doesn't) the company's mission statement and values align with what matters most to you in a future career?	
Would you be comfortable devoting your time and talents to help this company succeed? Why or why not?	
If you had to choose between these three types of employers, which type would you expect to enjoy working for the most? Why?	
Based on what you've learned through this process, what three factors have you identified as essential attributes of a future employer?	1 _____ 2 _____ 3 _____

Small Business	Government Agency
1 _____	1 _____
2 _____	2 _____
3 _____	3 _____

ADDRESS Options to Make the Most of Now

Well—big sigh of relief—you've almost made it through the entire Discover, Explore, Experiment process. This time and effort represent a huge investment in your future and has introduced a process you can rely on to guide you through a lifetime of career decisions.

But, you may well be wondering: "How do I get from here to there?"

Good question.

The answer? One step at a time.

No matter if you are moving full steam ahead toward a particular career or still meandering through the options—even if you are freaking out with indecision—here's what to do next: Map out a plan!

Your plan does not have to be set in stone with no wiggle room to take advantage of new opportunities. Instead it should move you forward along the pathway you choose to pursue and provide solid tools that prepare you to make the most of every opportunity that comes your way.

The first approach is complicated and, face it, a bit unrealistic. After all, who knows how your interests and talents will evolve over time? It's impossible to predict what kinds of as-yet-unheard-of opportunities will emerge in the future. Think about it. Did your great-grandparents dream of becoming computer programmers or Webmasters? Probably not. Chances are personal computers were an unimaginable innovation when they were making career choices. Long story short, the perfect career for you may not even exist yet.

The second approach is simple and leaves plenty of room for change as life and experience present new opportunities. It's not an attempt to plot out every last detail of your entire life. Instead, focus on making the most of now. What can you do now to get ready for a successful future? How can you get out of "stuck mode" and inch just a little closer to some actual choices?

The first thing you can do is to make the most of the opportunities waiting right under your nose for you to find them. These opportunities include wonderful new high school options designed to help students like you connect academic learning to real-world opportunities. Career academies, career pathways, career and technical education opportunities, and early college programs are just a few ways you can make the most of now.

Joining after-school clubs, volunteering for a cause you care about, and even getting a part-time job are other ways you can expand your horizons and gain useful experience. If it's information you are after, why not try some job shadowing or an internship at a local company of interest? Of course it goes without saying that getting good grades and staying out of trouble are helpful strategies, too.

There is so much you can do today to prepare for a brighter future. So why are you still sitting there? Start researching the options so you can map out a few next steps to get you where you want to go.

Next Step Options

X marks the spot. You are here in high school. How do you get from high school to a successful career? Find out all you can about various options offered at your school or in your community. Use the following checklist of options to keep track of details about each opportunity. You'll get a chance to map out specific next steps later.

OPTIONS

What kinds of career academies, career pathways, career and technical education, early college, or other special academic and career readiness programs does your school offer that fit with your career aspirations?

Ask your school adviser or guidance counselor to help you sort out which options are right for you.

What kinds of core academic courses can you take to prepare for a specific career pathway?

For instance, advanced math and science courses are good choices for someone looking toward a career in engineering.

What kinds of electives can you fit into your schedule to explore different kinds of opportunities?

For instance, environmental studies is a good choice for someone considering a green career.

What clubs and after-school activities provide opportunities to explore various career interests?

For instance, 4-H for someone interested in agriculture or natural resources; science competitions for future scientists; Future Business Leaders of America for business wannabes.

What local businesses offer opportunities for firsthand observations of how people do what you want to do?

Ask your school adviser or guidance counselor about job shadowing opportunities. Or go online to http://www.jobshadow.com to find out about local job shadowing opportunities.

What kinds of internship opportunities are available for students to get real-world work experiences?

Talk to your school adviser or guidance counselor about internship opportunities at your school.

Where can you volunteer to help further a favorite cause while, at the same time, building useful skills and experience?

Talk with the leader of a favorite community or religious organization about volunteer opportunities or go online to explore service learning options at http://www.learnandserve.gov.

What does your high school do to introduce students to various college, military, and other career training programs?

Ask your school adviser or guidance counselor for a schedule of college visits, career fairs, and other resources.

YOUR CHOICES

Academic and Career Readiness Programs

Core Academic Courses

Elective Courses

Clubs and After-School Activities

Job Shadowing Opportunities

Internships

Volunteer Experiences

College and Career Training Programs

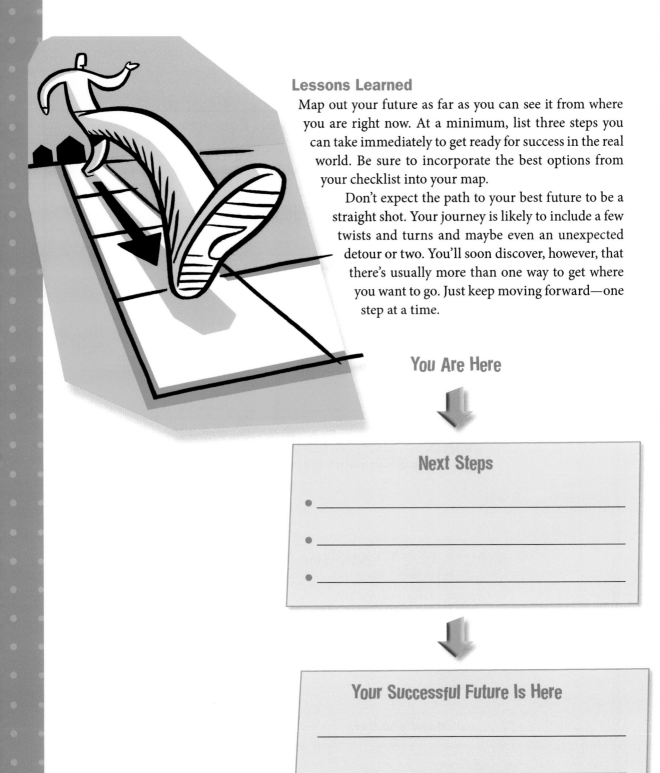

Lessons Learned

Map out your future as far as you can see it from where you are right now. At a minimum, list three steps you can take immediately to get ready for success in the real world. Be sure to incorporate the best options from your checklist into your map.

Don't expect the path to your best future to be a straight shot. Your journey is likely to include a few twists and turns and maybe even an unexpected detour or two. You'll soon discover, however, that there's usually more than one way to get where you want to go. Just keep moving forward—one step at a time.

You Are Here

Next Steps

- _____
- _____
- _____

Your Successful Future Is Here

_____

_____

A Final Word

Take a look back at all you've accomplished as you've worked your way through this book.

- You made important discoveries about yourself and the world of work.
- You explored a wide variety of career ideas found along this career pathway.
- You've experimented with three success strategies.

At this point, you may or may not be satisfied that you've got your future all figured out. Chances are you still aren't quite sure. Chances are even greater that things will change (maybe even more than once) before you put your big plans into action. After all, who knows what you'll discover as you get out there and experience the real world in new and interesting ways.

One thing is certain though: You are in better shape now than you were when you started reading this book. Why? Because you now have tools you can use to make well-informed career decisions—as you take your first steps toward your future career and throughout your life as you pursue new opportunities.

You've been wrestling with three big questions throughout this book.

- What do you know a lot about?
- What are you really good at doing?
- Where can you put that knowledge and those skills to work?

Rely on these questions to point you toward new opportunities as you move along your career path. Adjust them to reflect your constantly evolving experience and expertise, of course. And, whenever you find yourself in need of a career compass, simply revisit those questions again.

Then update that knowledge, hone those skills, and look for an employer who is willing to pay you to do what you really want to do!

With all this said and done, there's just one more question to ask: What *are* you going to do when you graduate?

Appendix

CAREER IDEAS FOR TEENS SERIES

Find out more about the world of work in any of these *Career Ideas for Teens* titles:

- *Agriculture, Food, and Natural Resources*
- *Architecture and Construction*
- *Arts and Communications*
- *Business, Management, and Administration*
- *Education and Training*
- *Finance*
- *Government and Public Service*
- *Health Science*
- *Hospitality and Tourism*
- *Human Services*
- *Information Technology*
- *Law and Public Safety*
- *Manufacturing*
- *Marketing*
- *Science, Technology, Engineering, and Math*
- *Transportation, Distribution, and Logistics*

VIRTUAL SUPPORT TEAM

As you continue your quest to determine just what it is you want to do with your life, you'll find that you are not alone. There are many people and organizations who want to help you succeed. Here are two words of advice: let them! Take advantage of all the wonderful resources so readily available to you.

The first place to start is your school's guidance center. There you will probably find a variety of free resources, which include information about careers, colleges, and other types of training opportunities; details about interesting events, job shadowing activities, and internship options; and access to useful career assessment tools.

In addition, there's a world of information just a mouse click away—use it! The following Internet resources provide all kinds of information and ideas that can help you find your future.

MAKE AN INFORMED CHOICE

Following are three especially useful career Web sites. Be sure to bookmark and visit them often as you consider various career options.

America's Career InfoNet

http://www.acinet.org

Quite possibly the most comprehensive source of career exploration anywhere, this U.S. Department of Labor Web site includes all kinds of current information about wages, market conditions, employers, and employment trends. Make sure to visit the site's career video library where you'll find links to more than 450 videos featuring real people doing real jobs.

Careers & Colleges

http://www.careersandcolleges.com

Here you'll find useful information about college, majors, scholarships, and other training options.

Career OneStop—Students and Career Advisors

http://www.careeronestop.org/studentsandcareeradvisors/
studentsandcareeradvisors.aspx

This Web site is brought to you compliments of the U.S. Department of Labor, Employment and Training Administration, and is designed especially for students like you. Here you'll find information on occupations and industries, internships, schools, and more.

GET A JOB

Whether you're curious about the kinds of jobs currently in big demand or you're actually looking for a job, the following Web sites are a great place to do some virtual job-hunting:

America's Job Bank

http://www.ajb.org

Another example of your (or, more accurately, your parents') tax dollars at work, this well-organized Web site is sponsored by the U.S. Department of Labor. Job seekers can post résumés and use the site's search engines to search through more than a million job listings by location or by job type.

Monster.com
http://www.monster.com
One of the Internet's most widely used employment Web sites, this is where you can search for specific types of jobs in specific parts of the country, network with millions of people, and find useful career advice.

Career Builder
http://www.careerbuilder.com
Another mega-career Web site where you can find out more about what employers are looking for in employees and get a better idea about in-demand professions.

EXPLORE BY CAREER PATHWAY

An especially effective way to explore career options is to look at careers associated with a personal interest or fascination with a certain type of industry. The following Web sites help you narrow down your options in a focused way:

All Career Clusters
Careership
http://mappingyourfuture.org/planyourcareer/careership
Find careers related to any of the 16 career clusters by clicking on the "Review Careers by Cluster" icon.

Agriculture, Food, and Natural Resources
Agrow Knowledge
http://www.agrowknow.org/
Grow your knowledge about this career pathway at the National Resource Center for Agriscience and Technology Education Web site.

Architecture and Construction

Construct My Future

http://www.constructmyfuture.com

    With more than $600 billion annually devoted to new construction projects, about 6 million Americans build careers in this industry. This Web site, sponsored by the Association of Equipment Distributors Foundation, Association of Equipment Manufacturers, and Associated General Contractors, introduces an interesting array of construction-related professions.

Make It Happen

http://www.buildingcareers.org

    Another informative construction-related Web site—this one sponsored by the Home Builders Institute.

Arts and Communications

My Arts Career

http://www.myartscareer.org

    Find out how to put your artistic talents to work at this Web site sponsored by the Center for Arts Education.

Business, Management, and Administration

Careers in Business

http://www.careers-in-business.com

    Find links to help you get down to the business of finding a career in business.

Education and Training

Careership

http://mappingyourfuture.org/planyourcareer/careership

    Find careers related to education, training, and library by clicking on the "Review Careers by Cluster" icon.

Finance

Careers in Finance

http://www.careers-in-finance.com/

    Find a wide variety of links related to careers in finance.

Government and Public Service

Public Service Careers

http://www.publicservicecareers.org

This authoritative Web site is cohosted by the National Association of Schools of Public Affairs and Administration and American Society for Public Administration.

Health Science

Campaign for Nursing Future

http://campaignfornursing.com/nursing-careers

Here's where to find information on nursing careers from A–Z.

Discover Nursing

http://www.discovernursing.com

More helpful information on nursing opportunities for men, women, minorities, and people with disabilities brought to you by Johnson & Johnson.

Explore Health Careers

http://explorehealthcareers.org/en/Field/1/Allied_Health
    _Professions

Find out about nearly 200 allied health careers at this informative Web site.

Hospitality and Tourism

O*Net Hospitality and Tourism Career Cluster

http://online.onetcenter.org/find/career?c=9

Visit this useful Web site to see career profiles about a wide variety of hospitality and tourism positions.

Human Services

Health and Human Services

http://www.hhs.gov

Explore federal health and human services opportunities associated with the U.S. Department of Health and Human Services.

Information Technology

Pathways to Technology

http://www.pathwaystotechnology.org/index.html

Find ideas and information about careers associated with all kinds of state-of-the-art and emerging technologies.

Law and Public Safety

National Partnership for Careers in Law, Public Safety, Corrections and Security

http://www.ncn-npcpss.com/

Initially established with funding from the U.S. Department of Justice, this organization partners with local and federal public safety agencies, secondary and postsecondary education institutions, and an array of professional and educational associations to build and support career-development resources.

Manufacturing

Dream It, Do It

http://www.dreamit-doit.com/index.php

The National Association of Manufacturers and the Manufacturing Institute created the Dream It, Do It campaign to educate young adults and their parents, educators, communities, and policy-makers about manufacturing's future and its careers. This Web site introduces high-demand 21st-century manufacturing professions many will find surprising and worthy of serious consideration.

Cool Stuff Being Made

http://www.youtube.com/user/NAMvideo

See for yourself how some of your favorite products are made compliments of the National Association of Manufacturers.

Manufacturing Is Cool

http://www.manufacturingiscool.com

Get a behind-the-scenes look at how some of your favorite products are manufactured at this Society of Manufacturing Engineers Web site.

Marketing

Take Another Look

http://www.careers-in-marketing.com/

Here's where you'll find links to all kinds of information about opportunities in marketing.

Science, Technology, Engineering, and Math (STEM)

Project Lead the Way

http://www.pltw.org

This organization exists to prepare students to be innovative, productive leaders in STEM professions.

Transportation, Distribution, and Logistics

Garrett A. Morgan Technology and Transportation Futures Program for Ninth through Twelfth Grade

http://www.fhwa.dot.gov/education/9-12home.htm

Get moving to find links to all kinds of interesting transportation career resources.

Index

Page numbers in **bold** indicate major treatment of a topic.